CW00765669

Benton End Remembered

Benton End Remembered

Cedric Morris, Arthur Lett-Haines and the East Anglian School of Painting and Drawing

compiled and edited by
Gwynneth Reynolds and Diana Grace
with a Foreword by
Richard Morphet

UNICORN PRESS
LONDON

Dedication

This book is to commemorate a special and unique place, a mecca for artists, gardeners, plant collectors, writers and creative people of many and varied talents. This I would like to celebrate. ***G.R.***

Unicorn Press
76 Great Suffolk Street
London SE1 0BL

email: unicorn@tradford.demon.co.uk

First published 2002 by Unicorn Press

ISBN 0 906290 69 4

Designed and typeset by Ferdinand Pageworks
Printed in Singapore by Compass Press Limited

Title page and book jacket (front): Cedric Morris: *Benton Blue Tit*, 1965. Oil on canvas. 72 x 64 cm. Private collection.

Contents

Acknowledgements vii
Foreword 1
Introduction 11
Index 159

Contributors

Glyn Morgan 15
Denise Broadley 23
Mollie Russell-Smith 27
Bernard Reynolds 33
Gwynneth Reynolds 41
Derek Waters 45
Ellis Carpenter 49
Kathleen Hale 53
Frank Pond 59
Robert Davey 63
Bernard Brown 65
Millie Hayes 73
Peter Wakefield 75
Felicity Wakefield 77
Michael Chase 79
Beth Chatto 83
Jenny Robinson 93
Janet Allen 97
Fiona Bonny 99
Frances Mount 103
Tony Venison 109
John Morley 113
Daphne Clark 117
Michael Lloyd 121
Maggi Hambling 127
Joanna Carrington 131
Anne Coghill 135
Ashe Ericksson 137
John Norris Wood 139
Elizabeth Wright 143
Ronald Blythe 149

Acknowledgements

We would like to thank all the contributors for their time, their valuable advice and their hospitality. Special thanks are also due to Maggi Hambling, Glyn Morgan and Richard Morphet for their encouragement and expertise; to our publisher, Hugh Tempest-Radford, for his faith in our project and to Brenda Herbert for her meticulous copy-editing. Any mistakes still remaining are our own. The following have also helped us in a variety of ways for which we are very grateful. Without them there would have been no book.

Douglas Atfield
Stephen Boswell
Beth Chatto
Julia Cubitt
Prudence Cuming Associates
Anne Blanco White and Richard Goodey of the British Iris Society
Barry Gooch
Mike Harding
Hugh Kelly
Jacqueline Korn of David Higham Associates Ltd
Nicholas McClean
S. P. McClean
Glyn and Jean Morgan
Jill and Laurence Ogden
Robert Short
Dorothy Sauvan Smith
Caroline and John Stevens
Alan and Anthea Stewart
The staff of the Archive Department, Tate Britain
The Trustees of the Cedric Morris Estate
Felicity and Peter Wakefield
David Wheeler of Bryansground Press
Katherine Wood and staff of firstsite@the minories art gallery, Colchester

Cedric Morris: *The River Brett, Hadleigh*. Oil on canvas. 69 x 61 cm. Minories

The following acknowledgements are also due for permission to reprint material from other sources:

Extracts by Kathleen Hale from *A Slender Reputation: an Autobiography*, Frederick Warne, London 1994. Illustrations by Kathleen Hale: Cedric as dancing master from *Orlando's Home Life*, Frederick Warne, London 1942; Lett as the Bowdlerised Katnapper from *Orlando (The Marmalade Cat) His Silver Wedding*, Frederick Warne, London 1944.
Article by Ronald Blythe 'Sir Cedric Morris' from *People, Essays & Poems* edited by Susan Hill, Chatto & Windus, London 1983.
Article by Beth Chatto 'Sir Cedric Morris, Artist-Gardener' from *By Pen & By Sword* an anthology from *Hortus: A Gardening Journal* No. 1 Spring 1987

Every effort has been made to trace the authors and publishers of material used and to acknowledge their contributions with gratitude. We apologise for any inadvertent omissions.

Foreword

Dating back several centuries, standing in walled gardens and overlooking the River Brett, Benton End was itself a significant part of the exceptional experience offered there between 1940 and 1982. Benton End's special enchantment in those years sprang, however, from the interaction between the setting, two remarkable individuals – Cedric Morris and Arthur Lett-Haines – and a pattern at once of work and of living that had Cedric and Lett at its centre.

The heyday of Benton End was the two decades from 1940, when the East Anglian School of Painting and Drawing was at its most active and the garden in its most concentrated period of cultivation. From the 1960s, the School's activity gently reduced and the garden, though still the site of continuous (and often important) plant breeding by Cedric, became less formal. But, despite these developments and Cedric and Lett's decline into old age, change came only in gentle stages. After the School ceased, its former students were often around, and even after Cedric stopped painting in 1975 and Lett died in 1978, Cedric's presence imparted a continuing character and vitality. Soon after Cedric died in 1982 the final step was the dispersal of the rarer plants. Benton End's magic was gone, but it is caught not only in art but also in the memory of those who knew it. Hence the importance of the recollections gathered here.

Cedric Morris: *Wartime Garden*, c. 1944. Oil on canvas. 59 x 75 cm. Private collection.

Eleven years before the move to Benton End, Cedric and Lett had taken a lease on a house some four miles distant, Pound Farm, near Higham (of which Cedric became the owner in 1932). Giving up a permanent London home, they lived there from 1930 and already their improbably colourful country lifestyle was established. Cedric's studio stood slightly above the beautiful sloping garden he developed, and The Pound witnessed a life of extraordinary animation, with legendary parties and a community of exotic birds. In 1937 Cedric and Lett established their art school in nearby Dedham, and it flourished there until accidentally destroyed by fire, less than six weeks before the outbreak of World War II. This disaster led to the School moving to Benton End and its becoming Cedric and Lett's home.

These moves and their timing created the circumstances that made life at Benton End so extraordinary during Cedric and Lett's first two decades there. For remarkable as life at The Pound had been, the consolidation at Benton End introduced two new factors. The School was now located in Cedric and Lett's house, and was also integrated

Cedric Morris: *Gutted Art School*, 1939. Oil on canvas. 65.5 x 81 cm. Minories

Lett Haines: *Old Brighton Railway Station*, 1920. Ink and watercolour. 47.5 x 62.5 cm. Private collection.

with its remarkable garden. Thus both the personal life of the two artists and the beauty of the garden (as well as the practical aspects of its management and Cedric's breeding of rare irises) became closely integrated, for students, with the process of creating art. Secondly, whereas during the years at The Pound Cedric still enjoyed a degree of metropolitan success, the years at Benton End coincided with his substantially disappearing from fashionable view. Indeed, his and Lett's suspicion of the commercial art world and its promotional pressures became entrenched in these decades. The energy they put into the work of the School was connected with this factor, for they sought to foster individual talent unbeholden to imperatives of style.

Thus not only was Benton End a kind of paradise, it also had the charm of being in a sense 'lost,' in terms of the London art world. To a degree it was cut off, too, from what was acceptable in its own non-metropolitan locality on the Suffolk/Essex border. For both

Cedric and Lett had once been avant-garde artists. The 'taint' still implicit in their relative modernity is exemplified by the elation voiced by Alfred Munnings, who lived nearby, as he was driven back and forth outside their art school in Dedham as the flames consumed it. In addition, the lives of Cedric, Lett and some of their students were anything but conventional. Benton End was thus regarded with a certain suspicion by some residents of Hadleigh, just beyond which it stood. Finally, although this unorthodox community was geographically in Suffolk, many have observed in how many respects its character was Mediterranean. In part, this was a consequence of Cedric and Lett's travels in France, Italy and North Africa, but by good fortune it was also the case that Benton End proved a benevolent habitat for many plants that in theory could thrive only in the southern countries from which Cedric brought them each winter after the war. In a household famous for its cosmopolitan cooking, one visitor was Elizabeth David, whose own love of Mediterranean food, likewise founded on having lived there, would help transform the eating habits of millions.

Cedric Morris by Bernard Reynolds.
Bronze. Private collection.

Complementing the strong colours of Benton End were the strong emotions at work in its small community. Though the dominant emotion was warmth, there was much drama. All these factors combined to give Benton End the character of a special, almost an enclosed world. Hence the unusual experience of first encountering it, even long after Benton End's richest period had ended. As I wrote shortly after doing so:

> To enter this circle was to enter a complete world, almost as if stepping into a novel. Everyone knew everyone else and had done so for decades, most of them had nicknames, and at the mention of Cedric and Benton End individuals turned radiant with a strange combination of joyous recollection and mischievous humour. Towards Cedric – and in many cases towards Lett Haines also – the attitude exceeded admiration and was one of intense devotion. No less apparent was the

Arthur Lett-Haines by Bernard Reynolds. Bronze. Private collection.

> extreme seriousness with which art itself was taken by all who were part of this circle. This blended quite naturally with their sense of fun and of extreme curiosity about individual behaviour. It would be difficult to imagine a circle in which art was more inextricable from its central subject, life.†

The dignity of the title 'The East Anglian School of Painting and Drawing' gives no hint of the unorthodoxy of the School's approach. In seeking to enable the student to realise his or her gifts to the fullest extent, its teaching was exceptionally undoctrinaire. Of key importance in the teachers' aspirations was that each student's way of working be sincere to their own vision. Thus, while soundness of technique was always fostered, aesthetic freedom was one of the School's keynotes. The pronounced contrast between the two principals' teaching methods also naturally tended to such an attitude. Cedric's involved few words and Lett's much theory. The two were united, however, in their commitment to the students' welfare.

Rather than an academy, the School was a community that in practice taught not only art but also the art of living. The exchange of ideas was a function of the fact that many of the students lived in, but also of the flow of visitors from the wider world, many of them active in fields other than art or horticulture. The additional vitalising ingredient provided by these visitors coexisted easily with the sense, described above, that Benton End was in many ways a place apart.

The absence of preconception in the School's teaching combined with its strongly pastoral tenor. These qualities help explain its description in one of its prospectuses as 'an oasis of decency for artists outside the system'. In turn, the phrase 'outside the system' links with many aspects of Cedric's self-perception, for example with his feeling of alienation from England by comparison with his native Wales

† In catalogue of Cedric Morris retrospective exhibition, Tate Gallery, London, March–May 1984, p 13.

(especially from what he saw as England's class system and its conventionality); with his strong Leftist commitment; with his homosexuality; with his preference for animals over people; and with his equal aversion from both the Academy and the post-1930 avant-garde. It connects also with the lack of distinction made by the School between professional and amateur artists, a feature that differentiated it from most art schools.

The multiple role of the garden at Benton End included contributing to the war effort, helping feed the students and providing motifs for painting. Cedric was an outstanding plantsman and a key category of visitor to Benton End was fellow specialists in this field. Cedric's greatest fame between 1940 and 1980 was not in art but as a breeder of irises, for which he won outstanding awards. At one time the garden contained around a thousand of his new iris seedlings each year and he painted his own irises annually. It was unusual for one of the principals of an art school to be celebrated in a discipline which, though distinct, he practised on the spot (and in which, moreover, in his non-prescriptive way, he was likewise a teacher). Cedric's attitude to flowers was, however, as unorthodox as that to art. He and Lett both saw strange and sometimes humorously impolite parallels between plant and human forms and were as aware of the savagery of plant life as of its often ravishing beauty.

The work of the school would not have been so enriching had not both extraordinary characters at its head been significant artists. Also important was the fact that their work as artists was as sharply unlike as they were as personalities.

Cedric's subjects were people, animals, birds, still life and landscape. Prominent among past art that he admired was that of Giotto, the Sienese school, Piero della Francesca, Holbein, Dutch still life painters of the seventeenth century, Stubbs, Goya, Audubon, Courbet, van Gogh, the Douanier Rousseau and Sickert, as well as Chinese painting. Common to all of these is clarity and directness, so

Cedric Morris: *Portrait of Eva Douglas*, 1926. Oil on canvas. 56 x 47 cm. Minories.

... both saw strange and sometimes humorously impolite parallels between plant and human forms ...

Cedric Morris: *Portrait of Helen Robbins*, 1936.
Oil on canvas. 64 x 48 cm. Minories.

Lett's work, by contrast, tended to complexity of both composition and meaning.

it is not surprising that Cedric disliked mannerism in any form. To quote again from the catalogue of Cedric's Tate retrospective.

> Early in his career [he] established a type of painting which remained essentially constant. Its principal feature is the extraordinary freshness – almost innocence – of his observation, and the directness with which he conveys to others the presence of any motif. His images range from ones of startling force to others of great delicacy, but they have in common a strange and effective use of colour, a powerful formal economy and reduction to essentials, and boldness in the juxtaposition of a picture's main subject with its background. Also very personal is [his] handling of paint, which he dabbed on thickly with the end of the brush, producing a rich and tactile texture.

Lett's work, by contrast, tended to complexity of both composition and meaning. His was a subtle and suggestive art, which emerged from ceaseless curiosity and from the continual impulse to experiment, even though his production was often interrupted for periods by the demands of helping others.

Both Cedric's and Lett's work in the 1920s was markedly advanced in a British context, but only in Lett's did the instinct to explore new idioms continue across the decades. As I have written about Lett's work previously, it:

> always has strange atmosphere which is peculiarly his own. His pictures are both amusing, enquiring and subversive. In them he speculates inventively but also restlessly, so that many of them have a quality which is almost disturbing – one of endless transformation. Lett's sinuous line not only states but suggests. Thus although one can almost always identify the animal or plant he puts before one, not only is it often far from apparent why it is found in its particular setting but no less frequently it seems to be turning before one's gaze into something else. Though Lett convincingly named Lewis, de Chirico, Kandinsky and Picasso as influences one is repeatedly reminded of the

> Surrealist metamorphosis of organic form, from Masson to Dali. Lett's rich paintings of flowers attest his love of beauty, but his works do not resolve into a state of calm. Surveying them, the sense builds up of one pursued … It is impossible not to admire the resilience with which his spirit of invention always re-emerged in new forms, continuing to the end of his life, when bold and expansive junglescapes were created in parallel with the tiny, mysterious, mixed-media *petites sculptures.*†

By the time Lett was making these late works, with their continued sense of fantasy, the calm and harmonious side of Cedric's vision was especially to the fore, in late paintings that employed a gentler palette than previously. Nevertheless, although the two artists' concerns contrasted throughout most of their careers, their art is linked by a certain quality of humour and subversiveness. Cedric also used painting, occasionally, as a mode of protest. As late as 1960 he could still paint a conspicuously angry picture, *Landscape of Shame*, a panorama of dead birds that indicted the harmful effect of pesticides. Such a work recalls his *Shags* of 1938, with its prophetic warning of the dangers of oil pollution, and his astonishing *Entry of Moral Turpitude into New York Harbour*, of 1926, which attacks the moral hypocrisy of the US immigration authorities. In targeting governments and large commercial/industrial organisations, such pictures demonstrate Cedric's resistance to accepted systems that curtail freedom of natural wellbeing. Related impulses underlay his deep engagement with Wales as when he was active in the disadvantaged communities of industrial south Wales and also worked for the development of indigenous Welsh culture throughout the Principality. The presence of Welsh artists was one of the enriching elements in the cultural mix of Benton End.

Both painters' early work shows the influence of Cubism and affinities with emerging Surrealism, but whereas these would long remain allegiances of Lett's they were quickly dropped by Cedric

† *Arthur Lett-Haines*, exhibition catalogue, Redfern Gallery, London, March-April 1984.

Cedric Morris: *Fascists in Rome*, 1922.

Cedric Morris: *Nemesis*. Oil on canvas, 53.5 x 44.5 cm. Minories.

(though not before he had made some remarkable abstract paintings). A longer-term pointer to the character of Cedric's art was his prominence in the Seven and Five Society, from 1926 to 1932. The leading painter members of this advanced Society at that time were linked by the freshness and simplicity of their imagery and the direct and frank way in which paint was applied. They included Winifred and Ben Nicholson (Cedric's proposers for Seven and Five membership), Christopher Wood, Ivon Hitchens and Frances Hodgkins. Cedric's work also shows affinities with aspects of the work of his near-contemporaries J.D. Innes, Derwent Lees and Dora Carrington, as well as with the landscape painting of John Nash (to whom he was close in his Suffolk years, owing to their shared interest in plants).

When exhibited by Peggy Guggenheim at her London gallery in 1938, some of Cedric's portraits were found outrageous enough to lead to violence. For more than twenty years from around 1920, the frontality, the psychological penetration and, again, the directness of these works show parallels with some art of the German *Neue-Sachlichkeit*.

One of the students of the East Anglian School of Painting and Drawing, both before and after its move to Benton End, was Lucian Freud, who enrolled at the age of sixteen. He has recorded his admiration of Cedric and his work, and the two painters' portraits of one another are in national collections. Despite major dissimilarities, their work is connected in its range of subjects, in the technique of moving steadily across the picture surface when painting, in the absence of mannerism and in the intensity with which the subject is scrutinised. A later Benton End student, enrolled at the still younger age of fifteen, was Maggi Hambling. In her case, the dominant influence was Lett, for while observation is vital for Hambling (as for Freud), her art is metamorphic in character and takes more than the material world as its subject. These affinities between teacher and student are reinforced by the parallels between the understated public presences of Cedric and of Freud and by Lett's and Hambling's notable shared gift for performing in front of groups of people.

Discussion of Benton End repeatedly makes reference to Freud and Hambling, owing to the unusually wide public recognition of their individual achievements. This is at once a credit to the extraordinary ambience created by Cedric and Lett and illuminating about the older artists' visions. But one factor that helped make Benton End so effective – even, no doubt, for Freud and Hambling – was the absence from its ethos of an urge towards fame and fortune. Thus the success of the enterprise should be measured, no less, by the fulfilment embodied in the work not only of other students who have achieved more than local recognition but also of artists little known outside the school's own circle.

Discussion of Benton End repeatedly makes reference to Freud and Hambling . . .

So many have testified that Benton End changed their lives. The experience it offered extended from the outdoor Cedric's reiterated emphasis on the special value of the natural to the indoor Lett's delight in the sophisticated and contrived. The two principal examples of human behaviour were Cedric's single-minded pursuit of his dual vocation as painter and plantsman and the complex Lett's tireless activity as the community's 'Father' and facilitator. The relationship between Cedric and Lett is at the heart of most of the recollections in this book, and the exceptional quality of Benton End is inconceivable without the contribution that each of them made. Ultimately it is their human qualities that made Benton End so remarkable. Their creativity and their partnership made possible in others a wide range both of achievement and of personal realisation.

Richard Morphet

Introduction

When Cedric Morris and Arthur Lett-Haines opened The East Anglian School of Painting and Drawing in Dedham, Essex in 1937 they were both established artists with international reputations. They had lived and worked in London, Cornwall and Paris, had travelled extensively and had made large numbers of friends among other artists. There had been a series of successful exhibitions in London and New York in the 1920s and Morris, in particular, had received critical acclaim and had sold a large number of paintings. His increasing disillusion with the commercial aspects of the art world, however, and Lett-Haines's determination to encourage his friend's work in congenial conditions were important factors in their decision to abandon London for the Suffolk countryside.

Their idea was to set up an art school which would provide an alternative to the formal courses offered by the art schools in the metropolis. The aim, as expressed in the school's brochure, was to provide 'an environment where students can work together with more experienced artists in a common endeavour to produce sincere painting'. The emphasis was on encouraging freedom of invention, enthusiasm, and enjoyment, with the assumption that the student 'believes himself to have a clear idea of creative work and requires help only in its production'. A further aim was 'to decrease the division that has grown up between the creative artist and the general public' and to that end, amateur artists were welcomed.

The School's early success, but also a disastrous fire which destroyed the Dedham building, necessitated a move in 1940 to larger premises at Benton End, Hadleigh in Suffolk, a house which had been unoccupied for fifteen years. There Cedric and Lett continued to live and work for the rest of their lives. The big, old, somewhat ramshackle house provided plenty of studio space as well as bedrooms for some of the students. The neglected grounds of three and a half acres were transformed gradually by Cedric into a wartime

Cedric Morris: *Garden Benton End*, 1944.
Oil on canvas. 59 x 75 cm. Private collection.

Some came to paint and sculpt, others to admire or help in the garden . . .

vegetable plot and later into a unique plantsman's garden full of bulbs, irises and roses which attracted visits from noted gardeners.

In addition to residential and day students, there were frequent visitors. Some came to paint and sculpt, others to admire or help in the garden, while many came to enjoy the welcoming atmosphere and the stimulating conversation of their friends. Although in later years Lett was unable to go on producing the gourmet feasts for the household which he had conjured up miraculously even during the war years, Millie Hayes, who joined the household in 1964, continued the great culinary tradition. Lett died, after a period of illness, in 1978, Cedric four years later at the age of ninety-two, bringing to an end a period of enormous creativity from which a large number of people lucky enough to have known[†] Cedric and Lett had benefited.

The extracts which form the text of this book are based largely on conversations with our contributors which took place during the years 1998 and 1999. Articles, extracts from an autobiography and a diary are also included. They comprise the affectionate memories of a few of those who knew and loved Benton End and its two gifted and hospitable hosts.

D.G.

[†] For a full account of Sir Cedric Morris's artistic career see Richard Morphet's Introduction to 'Cedric Morris' The Tate Gallery Catalogue of Retrospective Exhibition, 1984.

Glyn Morgan

Glyn Morgan first visited Benton End as a pupil in 1944 and continued to paint there for thirty-eight years. He has had numerous exhibitions and is represented in public and private collections in Britain and abroad. In 1985 he organised an exhibition of Benton End students' work at Bury St Edmunds' Art Gallery and in 1990 he was responsible for making a collection for the installation of a commemorative plaque on the wall of the house at Benton End.

My father said 'You're quite good with your hands. Why don't you become a garage mechanic?' However I managed instead to go to Cardiff Art School. I did the Illustration course because the Painting department only seemed to use black, dark green and khaki. It was a wise decision for this department was run by Ceri Richards, a wonderful draughtsman and inspiring teacher. Then in 1943 I met Cedric Morris, who had come to Pontypridd on one of his regular visits to Wales as a selector at a local exhibition for which I had entered some work. He liked my pictures and invited me to visit Benton End. I booked a week for the following summer and my life was changed.

The East Anglian School of Painting and Drawing, as Benton End was rather grandly called, was a large, shabby Tudor house just outside

Cedric Morris: *Café Rotonde*, 1922. Oil on canvas. 104 x 79 cm. Minories.

Cedric Morris: *Irises*. Oil on canvas. Private collection. 76 x 56 cm.

Glyn Morgan: *Species Irises*. Watercolour. Private collection.

... the air was heavy with the pungent scent of the flowers ...

Hadleigh, set in a very large garden full of horticultural treasures. I vividly remember my first evening there. A large scarred and studded zinc-covered table stood on the uneven brick floor. On the table an enormous pot of irises echoed a painting (now in Tate Britain) of the same subject on the wall; the air was heavy with the pungent scent of the flowers and the room roared with conversation and laughter. To a young man from the Welsh valleys the whole place was exotic and exciting. I think that this feeling of everything being larger than life was one of the main differences between Benton End and other summer schools. It was a world apart, where painting was the most important thing in life; for Cedric, I think, the only important thing except for his beloved plants.

There were no formal classes at Benton End. You started a picture in the studio or in the garden and after a while Cedric would amble up, his hands earthy, filling a foul old pipe from a battered ivory tobacco box. He never told anyone to use a particular technique. His criticisms were confined to the colour, balance and other basic formal qualities of the painting, so that while you wondered why you had not seen the solution before, the work remained *your* picture. Arthur Lett-Haines, known always as Lett, would also comment on one's work. His approach was more intellectual and he usually managed to contradict Cedric. Between the two of them we learned a lot. Lett had put aside his own painting in order to manage the house and look after Cedric. He was large and intimidating, malicious and warm-hearted and he produced two tremendous meals every day, to the accompaniment of loud and eloquent complaints and scurrilous comments on everyone he could think of. There was wine with both meals and after lunch everyone but the most determined workers staggered upstairs to sleep. Lett retired to his room and was not seen again until the evening, while Cedric often curled up in a flowerbed. The students usually prepared tea at about 4.30 pm except on Sundays, when it was always presided over by Lucy Harwood, an eccentric old lady totally dedicated to painting – and very good she was. She walked from her house in Layham carrying a basket of rather old buns and chunks of bread and jam, and ruled the tea table with a rod of iron. Her painting technique was very much her own. She would swing a loaded brush at the canvas as if attacking it and when she worked indoors the floor around her would be spread with newspapers to catch the splashes. Cedric, on the other hand, was much more deliberate. He would start at the top of the canvas and work his way in rows to the bottom, rather like knitting a pullover. His mastery of the medium was such that when he reached the bottom of the picture it never needed any alteration or adjustment.

He would start at the top of the canvas and work his way in rows to the bottom ...

One of the things that made Benton End such a rich experience was the wide variety of odd and interesting people it attracted. At one

Cedric Morris: *Garden Benton End* (Detail), see p. 12.

time there was a plague of psycho-analysts who covered the whole spectrum of behaviour from the highly intellectual to the downright crazy. One, who frequently threatened suicide, was known as Gas-oven Kate. Everyone had a nickname, usually invented by Lett. There was Hot-Handed Hetty or The Royal Bum, who was introduced to the house by me. She was very noisy and bursting with energy and would steal anything she fancied. However she made up for her short-comings by being a frequent and very drawable model. Lett made his presence felt all over the house, even when lurking in his room. It was widely accepted that he listened in to telephone conversations on the extension in his bedroom. This seemed a bit far-fetched to me but one day when my wife was coming to Benton End for the weekend I phoned her to give her directions for finding my room – she was arriving late – and I immediately heard Lett's heavy breathing on the line. I took no notice until I told her, 'Turn left on the landing.' 'No, right,' said Lett, followed by, 'Damn!' 'Thank you, Lett,' I said. No answer, but the heavy breathing continued, perhaps a little heavier by now. Neither Lett nor I mentioned it the next morning. I think he must have been embarrassed at being caught out, bless him.

Washing-up was done by the students and could be quite a chore if there had been a dozen or more people to dinner. It was not made easier by the general squalor of the kitchen. Every surface was covered with books, papers, bills and letters. The floor was cluttered with empty bottles and saucers for the cats and the old Aga, past its prime, cast an impartial film of coal dust over everything. The sink had to be seen to be believed. It was seldom empty and dreadful slimy dish-cloths lurked at the bottom of it. The wooden draining board had a spongy texture, but it is doubtful if this was a greater danger to health than the wooden plates, old and warped, and no doubt pulsating with germs. Luckily, Bryan Brooke, a celebrated proctologist, was a frequent student and was on hand to distribute quantities of Lomotil. In summer there were flies from the farm next door and tall

The sink had to be seen to be believed …

people had to be careful not to get their hair entangled in the fly-papers. At one stage an electric fly-killer was tried but this was not a great success. The flies used their last moments to escape into the dining room and expired there, dropping into one's lunch like rain.

I spent every available holiday at Benton End until I, like many others, began to feel that the creaking old house and the glorious garden were the only real life and the outside world was a sort of shadow-land. I never left without tears in my eyes. It is difficult to convey the magic of such a place in words, but I think it stemmed essentially from Cedric's personality. Why was he so much loved by so many people? I think mainly because he possessed a freedom of spirit that few achieve and this enabled him to give out unstintingly, expecting nothing in return but good manners and a commitment to work. His sense of humour was simple but robust. He had endless fun with his collection of seaside postcards with their shining, brightly coloured bosoms and bottoms, and we would often sit round the table until midnight laughing uproariously at things that would not have raised more than a smile at another time and place.

Cedric seems to have had the kind of public school education that makes very little impact on the intellect, but in any case his mind was completely intuitive rather than analytical. He was able to embrace wildly contradictory opinions without difficulty; he was a famous plantsman with a vast knowledge of the ways of nature, yet he thought that the Sizewell nuclear power station was going to blow up the world at any moment. He was an ardent socialist who could talk about the 'slave mentality'; he could compose a picture with the clarity and apparent ease of Mozart writing a sonata, but a screwdriver was to him an incomprehensible bit of high technology; he walked with a wilting, wincing step but could laugh at 'screaming queens'. He hated bores but was so charming to them that they kept coming back for more. He was outrageous, he was fun, he was a marvellous painter and certainly one of the great colourists of the century.

Cedric Morris: *Red Hot Pokers*, 1972. Oil on canvas. 89x 53 cm. Private collection.

He hated bores but was so charming to them that they kept coming back for more.

A personality like his does not easily leave a house that it has brightened for so long.

Cedric was spared most of the trials of old age, but the last few years of his life were shadowed by Lett's death and then by failing eyesight which eventually put an end to his painting. One can only imagine what this meant to him for he never complained. Only on one occasion did he remark that he regretted the pictures that he thought about but would never do. I don't think anyone fully realised that he had started to leave us some time before he died, so delicate and well-mannered was his withdrawal from the world. Sometimes it was apparent at breakfast time when I would hunt all over the room for his teeth, until he discovered with great merriment that he was wearing them. A personality like his does not easily leave a house that it has brightened for so long. The summer after he died I stayed again at Benton End to paint, and it seemed as if he might come into the studio at any moment. The next year I called once more. The house was just a house; the rooms seemed half the size. Cedric had finally gone.

Cedric Morris: *Denise Broadley*, 1934. Oil on canvas. 62 x 51 cm. Minories.

Denise Broadley

Denise Broadley, Sister Gillian CSC, was one of the first pre-war students at Higham, Dedham and Benton End. During the thirties she and Lucy Harwood toured Europe to paint. Although she was discouraged from painting during her period as an Anglican nun after the war, she started again while in Australia and has continued to paint and exhibit ever since at the New English Art Club, the Royal Academy and in local galleries.

I was one of the first students of the East Anglian School of Painting and Drawing in Dedham. I also went to the Westminster School of Art and lived and worked in London, but my family home was in Higham and I used to visit Cedric and Lett at The Pound. I introduced Barbara Gilligan, who had been at the Slade, to Cedric. Her home was in Suffolk and she took her paintings to The Pound for Cedric to see. Later Barbara married the artist David Carr.

Before the war, students and artists would gather at Bertorelli's or Beulah's in Charlotte Street. I met Cedric in London at a time when he was painting a lot of portraits and he did one of me.

Cedric bought a house for the School near to the mill in Dedham. Sir Alfred Munnings, who lived in Dedham, was in a state of fury about it. The Sun Inn in Dedham was a great meeting place; either

Lett or Cedric – I cannot recall which – painted the inn sign. Most of the students as well as models from London had lodgings in Dedham but they and other friends of Cedric and Lett would come to The Pound and we had some riotous weekends. Artists, actors and writers and people like John Skeaping, the sculptor, would be there. Lucian Freud turned up in 1938 or 1939 from Dartington and lived in the School. He did a very good drawing of me and called it 'Denise and all her Suitors' because of all the figures of male students in the background. Lucian Freud was there when the building burnt down and he always felt responsible for the fire.

I did a lot of drawing at Dedham and I also used to take myself off into the countryside to paint. Lett was particularly brilliant at drawing and teaching. He would show you a line or a curve and it was always exactly right. He worried that when I went to Westminster they would ruin me. Lett was the backbone of the organisation of the School and it was he who ordered all the art materials, although there was a secretary, the wife of a local architect. Lett would sometimes come in while Cedric was helping me with my painting and Cedric would be furious and send him away. Lett would get offended.

Cedric would say very little. Maybe he would push his thumb at something and say, 'Well, that there is out of tone. It will only take a minute.' Of course it took me much longer. He would tell you if there was something wrong but he was never destructive. I took all the criticism and worked to get it right. Occasionally he would say, 'Oh, that's a beauty,' and once he said, 'Congratulations, a wonderful lot.' He had a marvellous overall view of a picture. Cedric was good at teaching technical things you would never learn at art school like how to make canvases and paints. We would buy coach paints and mix our colours.

He would tell you if something was wrong but he was never destructive.

Cedric didn't drive so one day I drove him to John Nash's at Wormingford for tea and I mentioned that I wanted someone to go

Cedric Morris: *Lucy Harwood*, 1941. Oil on canvas. 66 x 51 cm. Minories.

abroad with. An artist called Celia Bedford was there and she offered to go with me. Our first trip was to Bruges. I also went several times to Paris and Brittany with Lucy Harwood. We would stay in convents and paint and we painted in the streets in Paris. I would bring back all my work from these trips to Dedham.

After the war I taught art at a convent in London and joined the community there in 1950, which upset Cedric but I needed the security after trying to manage living in London with only unqualified teacher's pay every three months. Because I was teaching full time in London I couldn't go much to Benton End but much later I went to find all my old paintings and drawings which had been stowed away in a cupboard.

Benton End was always full of people. Once there were lots of women doctors and shrinks and a rector from London who told Cedric he should give all his paintings to the Church. People used to lodge in the cottages nearby and Lucy used to take in the more respectable visitors. Not everyone liked Benton End – Maudie (Joan Warburton) said that they never did any work there!

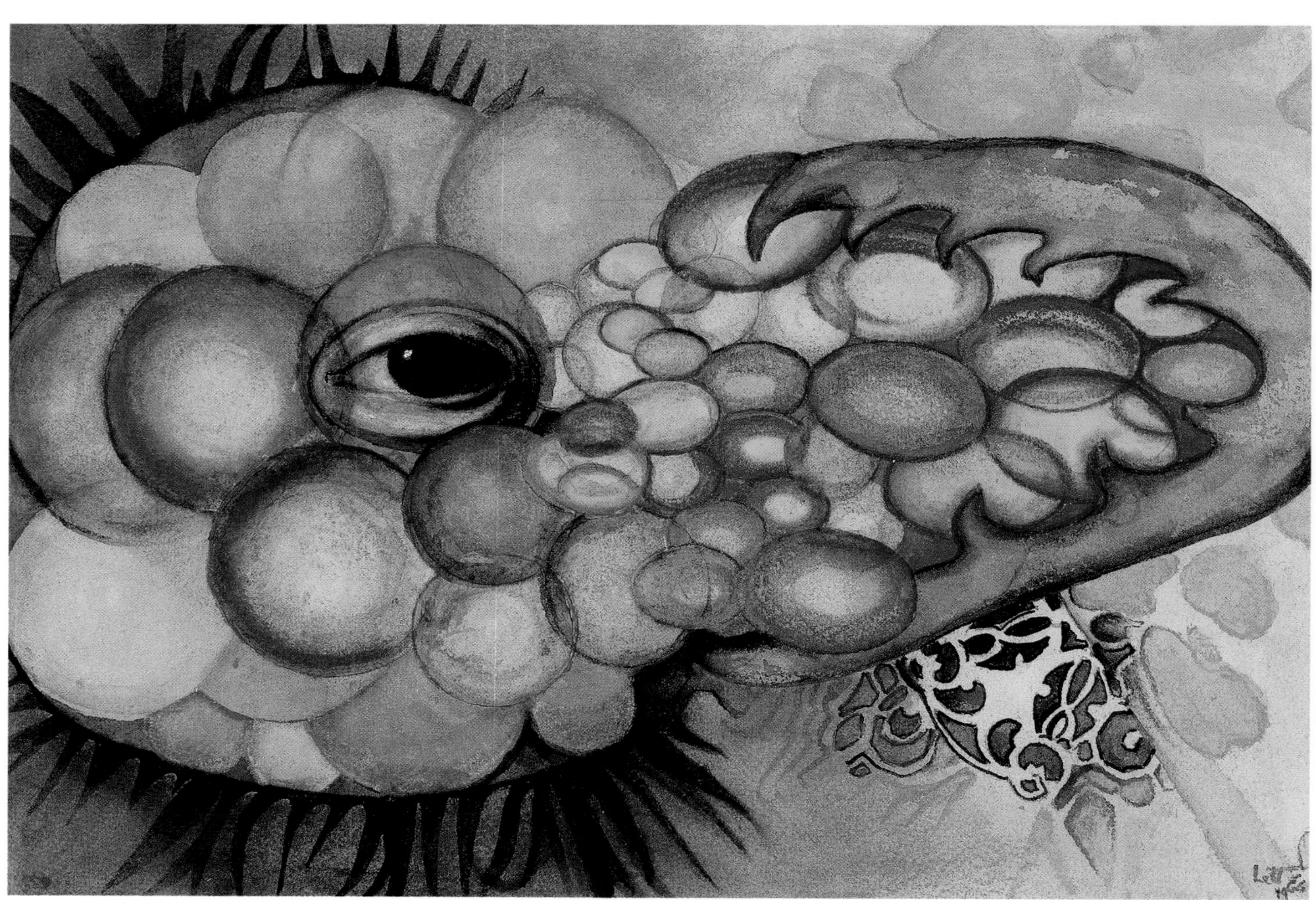

Mollie Russell-Smith

Mollie Russell-Smith was born in Hertfordshire with Suffolk roots and is a painter, printmaker, poet and teacher. She was married first to John Frost, singer and composer, and then to Eric Lungren, a dedicated gardener, whose flowers were often an inspiration for prints and paintings. She studied at the Beckenham School of Art before arriving at Benton End. Mollie has now retired from teaching and is living in Beckenham where she still paints, prints and writes.

During the war my mother, brother and I left our bomb-damaged home for the safety of my aunt's cottage in Hadleigh. I was an impoverished art student, uprooted from the Beckenham School of Art and transferred to the one at Ipswich.

In the summer holiday I was bemoaning the fact that I had no easel and a neighbour suggested that I try 'those nice people in the artist's house' who might lend me one. So with much trepidation I walked down to Benton End and knocked on the front door. It was flung open by three young men – Dickie Chopping, Dennis Wirth-Miller and Lucian Freud. They bundled me in, assuming that I had come to be a student, and Dickie showed me all over the house with great enthusiasm and charm. I was enchanted. The house with its bare floors and simple furnishing was alive with colour, crammed

Lett Haines: *Congrès sur l'oeil*, 1965. Mixed media. 38.7 x 26.2 cm. Private collection.

with paintings and exotic objects. No one else was about but the young men said, 'You must see Father. Come and see Father tomorrow and bring some work.' I went away bemused. I had been too shy to mention the easel.

The next day I returned with my folio and some paintings and found Father, who turned out to be called Lett, in the kitchen. He looked at my work and asked me when I wanted to start. I explained that there was some mistake as I already had a place at Ipswich Art School. 'How much do you have to pay?' he asked. I replied, 'Nothing; it's like a kind of scholarship.' 'In that case,' Lett said, 'we will have to give you a scholarship here and for your keep you can have a job helping me in the kitchen.' Two days later I moved in and stayed as a live-in student for about two years.

Cedric Morris: *Still Life with Courgettes and Tomatoes*, 1957. Oil on canvas. 77 x 104 cm. Private collection.

Kathleen Hale … was handsome, dynamic and bawdy …

Although it was war-time we ate very well for Cedric grew every sort of vegetable in the garden, including special ones like asparagus and globe artichokes. There was an excellent herb bed. The orchard yielded plenty of fruit and there we kept chickens and geese as well as a goat with her kid, named Little Billy. There was often a strong smell of chicken being cooked on the Aga. Lett's cooking was imaginative and cosmopolitan. Nothing was wasted: pigs' heads were cooked to make brawn and there was always soup simmering on the Aga into which Lett once knocked his packet of cigarettes. They were fished out and dried over the stove. All peelings and scraps went into a bucket to mix with the hens' meagre corn ration. Cedric also supplemented his tobacco ration by growing his own. The leaves hung drying in the apple room. Eventually we had to eat Little Billy. Cedric stretched the skin and one of his students tried to cut a waistcoat for him. The hide, though, was not big enough so I rescued the cuttings and I made myself a beautiful white fur hat.

Life at Benton End was strange in that often it was empty save for Cedric, Lett and me and then suddenly we would be invaded by masses of visitors. Apart from students coming for short stays to paint, there were people coming for weekend leaves from the forces. Maudie (Joan Warburton) would appear in her Wren's uniform and Denise (Broadley) in her Land Army breeches. David Carr stayed for some weeks and managed to get a permit to paint at Ipswich Docks, which at that time was a restricted area. Lett's mother descended wearing her Red Cross uniform – she was a formidable lady. I once heard her say to Lett, 'Arthur, there are times when I don't like you. This is one of them!' John Skeaping visited and so did Matthew Smith. I met countless artists and plant enthusiasts and made friendships that lasted for years.

Kathleen Hale, known as Moggie or Mog, often stayed at Benton End, both as an accomplished artist and as Lett's mistress. She was handsome, dynamic and bawdy and I was very fond of her. She took me to Ipswich to Cowells, her printers, where I was able to view the lithographic plates from which her drawings for *Orlando the Marmalade Cat* were printed. She was very good to me and got me portrait and illustration commissions.

In spite of the war it was quite a happy time. There were dances at the Town Hall and lots of parties at friends' houses and at the local Officers' Mess. Lett and Cedric were always hospitable to whoever turned up, whether it be a mandarin from the Arts Council or a GI airman from the camp up the road. The evening meals that Father cooked were delicious, with many dishes of great variety. We sat round the candle-lit table talking for hours. Both Lett and Cedric had their own quirky sense of humour and conversation was a delight. Sometimes we played records on the wind-up gramophone: Walton's Facade with Edith Sitwell speaking her poems, Mozart, Bach, Constant Lambert and Douglas Byng.

We sat round the candle-lit table talking for hours.

Summer at Benton End was idyllic. Cedric cultivated his wonderful flowers and everywhere was suffused with scent and light. But the winters were bitterly cold and the house had little heating. Cedric, Lett and David Carr all wore thick Aran sweaters. Cedric had warm shirts of Welsh flannel and tough corduroy trousers fastened with a leather belt with an ornate Mexican silver buckle. His long, black, woollen cloak hung conveniently in the hall where it got borrowed both by Lucian and me. I remember at one time Lucian acquired a scarlet military tunic (anticipating sixties fashion by twenty years) much to the amazement of the locals.

As an art school Benton End was unique. There was no formal teaching and instead students would show their paintings for criticism to Lett in the kitchen or Cedric in the garden. I learned to paint and draw in a very direct manner. In fact both my art and my life were influenced profoundly by Cedric and Father whom I loved dearly. I became more passionate about colour. Lett once said that next to Matisse, Cedric was the finest colourist this century. From

Cedric Morris: *Iris, Poppies and Clematis*, 1940. Oil on canvas. 91 x 121 cm. Private collection.

Cedric I learned to use colour to define the form rather than being overly concerned with the source of light. Also the sense of place – maybe I always had that; it's just that at Benton End one's own intuitions were valued. From Lett I learned to appreciate the happy accident and to grasp the moment whether in art or in life. Lett was not only a great raconteur but also a delightful poet. He taught me a lot about writing for which I am eternally grateful.

For some years after leaving Benton End I was unable to visit, but when I did return the place still held its old magic. However as Lett and Cedric grew older things became run down. Cedric's eyesight deteriorated and Father's health failed. The last time I saw Father he, who rarely ventured into the garden, was reclining under a tree enjoying the sun. I kissed him goodbye. Smiling he lay back and suddenly, cocking his feet in the air said, 'Growing old's a bugger, dear. I don't recommend it.'

'Growing old's a bugger, dear. I don't recommend it.'

Bernard Reynolds

Bernard Reynolds studied at Norwich and Westminster Schools of Art. During 1937–8 he was associated with Henry Moore and contributed to The Surrealist Object exhibition at the London Gallery. He was lecturer in charge of 3D studies at Ipswich School of Art until 1981. Bernard Reynolds convened a number of East Anglian Sculpture exhibitions and exhibited sculpture and drawings widely in Suffolk, Essex and Norfolk. He executed several public commissions in Norwich and Ipswich, including his Ship Fountain in Ipswich Civic Centre which won the Sir Otto Beit Medal. His bronzes of Sir Cedric Morris and Arthur Lett-Haines can be seen in Christchurch Mansion, Ipswich. Bernard Reynolds was a Fellow of the British Society of Sculptors. The following extract is from his diary of 1945.

May 9

The East Anglian School of Painting and Drawing is based in a Georgian-fronted Elizabethan house, Benton End, which is part pink lime-washed and part half-timbered and herringbone brickwork. Cedric Morris I find to be a very charming fellow, perhaps more famous as an iris culturist than as a painter. He runs the spacious gardens packed with most gorgeous and unusual flowers and most of

Lett Haines: *Pigmy Pouter Pigeons*, 1930. Mixed media. 55 x 45 cm. Private collection.

his paintings are of flowers. I have already had some arguments with Cedric about design. He says you cannot use horizontals in a picture without at least breaking them up or losing them before they reach the side of the canvas. I am yet to be convinced.

'The Lord doesn't provide ready-made designs . . .'

Arthur Lett-Haines runs the catering and business side of the place, not through choice but 'because no help can be got in war time'. Lett complains that Cedric is a contrary and stubborn dreamer who won't help a bit about the place, whereas he himself would love to paint but his time is spent in endless cooking and washing-up. In a fortnight's time, says Haines, the iris fanciers will flock to Hadleigh to see Cedric's rows and rows of show irises and they will all have to be fed and bedded by Lett himself. (The irises are only in bud at present except for some dwarf black specimens.)

Lett Haines cooked a marvellous evening meal: roast lamb, onion sauce, braised chicory and mashed potatoes and parsley. This was followed by fruit-wine jelly with sauce that tasted like raspberry ice cream. Black coffee with saccharin. After this Lett took me down to the local for a pint of bitter and asked me all about myself.

I just couldn't sleep at all – it was the coffee, the beer, the late, heavy meal and the heat. There was a colossal beetle flying round the room making a noise like a vibro-massage machine and drowning out the song of a nightingale out of doors.

May 13

I selected a typical Morris subject, some tulips growing in the garden, and had to fit them into a preconceived design because I couldn't find any groups forming a design. When I mentioned to Morris that normally I would have cut the tulips and arranged them in the pot, he said, 'Good God, man, you can't rearrange the landscape on the earth's surface; you have to rearrange on your canvas! The Lord doesn't provide ready-made designs – Gawd don't hold with this 'ere Art.' However, having painted the tulips in their relatively balanced

Cedric Morris: *Plant Design*, 1927. Ink and watercolour. 37 x 29.5 cm. Private collection.

positions, I had to think of some subject to provide a background, linking the blooms and creating some recession, but just as I decided on a nearby landscape, the gong went for lunch. The morning had been a scorcher and I could hardly stand the blazing sun as I painted the tulips. In the afternoon a strong breeze got up and I had to tie my canvas firmly to the donkey. Even so, the wind buffeted my palette and deflected my brush. Altogether a day of mental torment and indecision but offering original and exciting concoctions to eat, especially in view of the strict rationing. Chinese fare and coffee-chocolate blancmange for lunch and for supper an elaborate salad, then fruit sundae and ice cream. Lett certainly can cook!

Lett certainly can cook!

May 14

Started with gusto painting in the background to the tulips but found it difficult. The slim stems were sparse compared with the background landscape and it was a problem to integrate the two. I struggled with it all morning and the latter part of the afternoon but after all decided to abandon it. I shall not destroy it though because the tulips are well painted and I may be able to save it yet.

Several people arrived after lunch, among them Frank Pond and 'Minnie' (Jasmine Gordon-Forbes, Art Editor in the Ministry of Propaganda in Europe). After supper a brisk discussion of art principles ensued. I expressed some of my recent discontents and they were met very charmingly by Cedric. This was the first bit of really stimulating social intercourse and the creative urge developed immediately so I decided I would paint the big bunch of irises standing on the table nearby. I just had time to set out the main lines of the composition before bedtime.

May15

I am a little disappointed with the painting but when I communicated my despair to Cedric he said, 'Now now, don't get hysterical.' I

Cedric Morris: *The Minton Pot*, 1955. Oil on canvas. 76 x 50 cm. Private collection.

thought it was coming out rather like an art school study, too academic, but Cedric said he liked it which encouraged me to carry on.

The more I talk to Cedric the more I appreciate him. He is a proper cowboy in appearance with big brown leather jacket and wide corduroy trousers buttoning up at either side and a red neckerchief worn with a toggle. We have discussed all aspects of art, painting and sculpture, primitive to modern, and I follow most of his ideas but am beginning to realise that I know nothing about colour. I have always considered it an adjunct to light and shade. Cedric uses very little light and shade and considers colour for its own emotional sake. Thus I am hearing for the first time students being shown, say, 'how to make that peculiar green of the tulip leaves' or 'No, I should use terre verte there, painted over a black background – it is more transparent than chrome/cobalt green mixed with black'. To me colour is a matter of mixing the primaries, red, yellow, blue, but to Cedric much is concerned with the inherent nature of individual pigments. He told me that a colourist was a man who thought creatively in terms of colour, that is he was continually discovering how to make new colours and that is why his paintings, like Lett's cooking, have extraordinary yet exquisite colour-flavours which cannot be analysed into their constituents.

Lett is a thoughtful, generous and fatherly man and treats all his students as his children, although some may be in their forties. He is an extremely good critic and helpful instructor, but I hate his voice – everything he says is announced to the world and if he is having a 'quiet' talk with the cleaning lady about her sciatica or a prolonged grumble about the tradesmen in the town it can be heard several rooms away. On the other hand, Cedric talks very quietly, usually in good humour punctuated with little chuckles. Occasionally he comes out with some surprising ruderies which prolong the chuckles. He seems a happy soul generally but one can detect a certain rift between him and Lett. Lett never appears at meal table with Cedric and guests; Cedric never ventures into the kitchen. Lett does not join in art discussions; they have separate rooms and studios.

May 16

Inspired by Cedric's colour theories I have started an experimental painting of a white iris against a lichen-covered wall. I have to think of a way to relate the iris to the wall and I expect to do this with a shadow. At present I have just painted the bricks; later I will add the lichen and when this is dry, the iris.

One of the local boys (they continually invade the place and Cedric hasn't the heart to turn them away although they do some damage) brought a duckling he had poached from a nearby farmer. He carried it inside his shirt! Cedric, instead of asking the boy how he came by it and scolding him, was delighted, advising him on how to make a run and nest box, how to feed it and he offered to look after it until the boy was ready. So now we have a box in the studio.

May 17

Another glorious day without a cloud in the sky, most unusual for May. Marvellous flowers in bloom, more every day. A peacock butterfly and at dusk, white ermine and buff ermine moths. I have a great accord with Cedric for we can talk modern French and English painters and sculptors and also about moths, butterflies, fungi and wild flowers. Lett, on the other hand, indulges in gossip and wildly exaggerated anecdotes about people. This is quite outside my field of thought and I tend to escape.

On the subject of colour, Cedric was saying today that sometimes in commencing a flower painting he will start by covering the canvas with two extraordinary colours which clash in violent discord. He will then select flowers or other subjects which will bridge the gap and bring about a certain harmony yet preserve a vibrant set of relationships.

'Paint what you like but paint it well.'

May 18

I have just finished the Iris and Wall and the larger composition of irises. I do not seem to have 'burst my bodice' as Lett would say.

May 22

'Every painting should be a further experiment in the organisation of colour.'

My last day. I left Hadleigh, in pouring rain incidentally, and feeling that I had produced nothing in the least satisfactory but I have learned a lot and enjoyed the social and intellectual stimuli. Morris says, 'Paint what you like but paint it *well*. Good painting means rich, fluent painting. Look at Picasso, look at Matisse or if you must come nearer home, look at Constable or at Matthew Smith. Every painting should be a further experiment in the organisation of colour. Do not weaken all your colours by adding lots of white – keep them rich like the French do. Only use white as a colour, to mix with red to make pink or to paint a white object. Mix your white with other pigments on the palette and never on the canvas as this will make the painting look chalky.'

The most interesting part of the discussions with Cedric and Lett was to hear their personal opinions on leading painters of our time and their yarns about such artists in London, Paris and New York. They seem at least to have been in the presence of Picasso, Matisse, Derain and Léger and they became great friends with the Russian-born sculptor Ossip Zadkine who had visited them in Suffolk. I was glad to discover that Cedric agreed with me that Léger was no artist at all and Derain was hard and clumsy and unable to judge his successes from his failures. He thought that Matthew Smith had the latter failure too.

Oh well, lots to think about for a long while ahead.

CEDRIC MORRIS

Cedric Morris: *Cabbages*, 1953. Oil on canvas. 95 x 117.5 cm. Private collection.

Gwynneth Reynolds

Gwynneth Reynolds is a past student of the East Anglian School of Painting and Drawing. This book is the result of her desire to capture the memories of some of the many friends and students who knew and loved Cedric and Lett and the world they created at Benton End.

I was born on Teesside. My father was a teacher and my mother had been a nurse during World War I. My family was not particularly artistic. The only paintings I can remember in my home were reproductions of *When did you last see your father?* by W. F. Yeames and *The Boyhood of Raleigh* by J. Everett Millais.

At the age of sixteen I left school to begin a nursing career. The hours were long, the work was hard and the food dreadful. Still, I was very lucky to make a good friend in another nurse, Liz Maufe, the niece of the architect Sir Edward Maufe who designed Guildford Cathedral. In our spare time we would go off painting and sketching in Wharfedale. Liz's uncle had designed the family home on the wild and remote edge of the moors. I spent wonderful holidays there. It was a revelation for me to see for the first time original watercolours and oil paintings and hand-thrown mugs and bowls. We danced on the terrace to music from a wind-up gramophone wearing dirndl skirts and twirling chiffon scarves in the manner of Isadora Duncan.

We felt very 'arty', free and bohemian (a word hardly ever used now). It was a great contrast to the grim realities of wartime nursing in wards full of casualties – young men with amputations and spinal injuries, many hopelessly mutilated and many dying.

Art was a great relief and escape so I enrolled for an evening class, where I remarked to a woman in the class how I would love to spend more time drawing and painting. As the class dispersed she handed me a slip of paper with the address of the East Anglian School of Painting and Drawing in Hadleigh, Suffolk and said I would like it there. After I had completed my nursing training I literally 'got on my bike' for Benton End by putting my bike in the guard's van and setting off cross-country to Ipswich.

I arrived at Benton End to find a party in full swing. It was summer and the garden was lush and exotic. The food was varied and lavish, a great contrast to the canteen food I had become used to and there were flowers and wine. People drifted around in groups or lounged in the shade. Of course I had no idea who anyone was but it was a magical moment, rather strange and surreal as if I had stepped into another world. I had become very institutionalised in my Birmingham hospital.

Next day, as overnight guests and hangers-on departed I was surprised to realise that only one student remained and even he soon left. At first I felt disappointed, having expected a lively throng of young people. As I settled in, however, and began to paint, I absorbed the wonderful atmosphere – the peace and quiet so different from hospital routine. At meal-times there was always marvellous Mediterranean food with fish and sea-food, lovely garden produce and wine. The conversation was unusually free and sometimes bawdy, but as I was very naïve it often went above my head.

The conversation was unusually free and sometimes bawdy …

The teaching at Benton End was very informal. I was left to my own devices to wander in the garden and set up my easel. Cedric would quietly appear, put his head on one side and say, 'Yes … well,'

... dreadful wooden draining board, wooden plates and woollen underwear steeping in bowls.

and perhaps make suggestions about the composition. He warned me about over-using viridian green, suggesting that I might mix lamp black with yellow ochre to get sap green or mix zinc powder from the chemist's with linseed oil rather than buy zinc white. Lett, who called me 'Tiny Child', hardly ever appeared in the garden, though I remember one occasion when he appeared, looked at my painting and said, 'Ah! We have a Monet here.' He was given to wild exaggeration! The other students who came in the afternoons seemed elderly to me. There was Lucy Harwood who brought cake and made tea, Mildred Blakiston and Joan Warburton (Maudie). At weekends the gardeners and London people would arrive.

When my money ran out and I could not afford to stay on Lett suggested that I might lodge at The Pound, a house owned by Cedric about two miles away, and he drove me to meet the tenants, Bod and Tom (Tom and Elizabeth Wright). It was idyllic in that Elizabethan timber-framed house set in a valley and I stayed till the end of the year, painting and earning money fruit-picking. Cedric suggested that I should submit some of my work to the Colchester Art Society Exhibition and I was proud to see it hanging next to paintings by John Nash, Cedric Morris and Rowland Suddaby.

It was while I was at The Pound that I met my future husband Bernard, who was head of sculpture at Ipswich School of Art. After I married and had children I saw less of Cedric and Lett. I was too busy and anyway Benton End was not a particularly suitable place to take children. Years later, however, I took over the kitchen when Millie, the housekeeper, was on holiday. The kitchen was absolutely primitive with an ancient Aga with the inside hanging out which needed constant stoking. There was a deep stone sink, dreadful wooden draining board, wooden plates and woollen underwear steeping in bowls. Lett by that time was far from well and no longer did the cooking. He spent a lot of time in bed and needed a special diet and various medications. I realised how hard it was for Millie to work in these conditions yet still manage to produce excellent meals. Nevertheless I did enjoy doing the cooking in spite of the hard work. Spearings of Dedham, 'the Harrods of East Anglia', delivered wonderful supplies and there were superb fruits and vegetables in the garden. I would stew fruit in honey and spices overnight in the slow oven. All the time I was aware of the need to balance my attention between Cedric downstairs in his studio or in the garden and Lett upstairs. The two men led a bachelor lifestyle with no comforts, not even easy chairs or proper heating, though in the winter the house was locked up and Cedric and Lett went their separate ways abroad.

As the years passed Bernard and I would visit Benton End to talk to Cedric and Lett. Cedric was of course to be found in the garden and Lett either resting in his room or in his studio. We might mention to Lett some social occasion at Wivenhoe which was at that time a focal point for artists. Francis Bacon had a studio there, Denis Wirth-Miller and Richard Chopping lived there and George Gale had converted the outbuildings of his large house as an art club. Lett always showed interest so we often arranged to take him with us. He would dress for the occasion like an Edwardian dandy in striped trousers, starched white shirt and patent leather shoes, carrying a black walking-stick with a silver knob. He often looked tired and the old sparkle had gone but he never missed a chance to go out and about. The ladies always made a fuss of him and he usually had a dance or two.

Benton End changed my life and the lives of many others too.

Cedric Morris: *Daya Majorca* (Detail),. Oil on canvas. 60.5 x 48 cm. Minories.

... in the winter ... Cedric and Lett went their separate ways abroad.

Derek Waters

Derek Waters was brought up in Hadleigh. His association with Benton End began when he was twelve and lasted until Cedric's death. Derek Waters' career was in lithography. He continues to paint for pleasure.

My long association with Benton End began in 1941 when I was 12 years old. Cedric and Lett had moved to Hadleigh in 1940 where they reopened the East Anglian School of Painting and Drawing after the Studio in Dedham had been destroyed by fire in 1939. My father had met Lett in our local public house and told him of my interest in drawing and painting. Lett suggested that I take my artwork to the School and he and Cedric would give their opinion. Having decided that I had a natural talent, Lett asked that in exchange for instruction from him and Cedric in the evenings I should light the kitchen stove, make the early morning tea and prepare the breakfast table. Elizabeth David, who often stayed at Benton End as guest and friend and who discussed food preparation with Lett, kindly gave me helpful advice for this task.

Cedric's teaching methods were really quite straightforward, quite unlike that of the usual art school, and had evolved from his admiration of the Impressionists and from the fact that he was largely self-taught. He felt that a sense of freedom in painting was essential. He was very open and left people to develop their own style of painting and drawing. When I felt that I had got as far as I could with a painting Cedric would sit with me discussing the importance of composition, draughtsmanship, colour, recession, where objects appeared in the painting and the necessity of correct positioning. With such in-depth and free discussion I think people developed their latent talents quickly without working one stage at a time. We students were all encouraged by Cedric to exhibit at Colchester Art Society shows.

... people developed their latent talents quickly ...

During the evenings at Benton End I met many interesting people, friends and students staying with Cedric and Lett. There was another local lad, Tommy Wright, who some years later married Elizabeth Bodman. There was Kathleen Hale, the author, who during her visit wrote some of her *Orlando the Marmalade Cat* stories, using Lett as her model for the cat burglar and me as the running boy. It was Kathleen who suggested lithography as a career for me, promising to speak to the managing director of the printing firm W. S. Cowell, Ipswich, on my behalf, so at the age of fourteen I began my lithography career which was to last fifty enjoyable years, interrupted only by two years of national service. I started by drawing on zinc plates and later went on to electronic scanning.

Throughout this time I continued my close association with Benton End, meeting people such as Bernard Evans, Mollie Russell-Smith, Lucian Freud, David Keay, Ernest 'Constant' Constable, Hattie Shelton, Renata Fisher, Lucy Harwood, Esther Grainger, Glyn Morgan, Kitty Epstein, Annie Goossens (a member of the musical Goossens family) and the sculptor Bernard Reynolds. I am still in touch with Denise Broadley, visiting various gatherings to give support when she has an exhibition. Millie Hayes became a permanent member of the household some years after the war, helping Lett with the cooking and the organisation of the School. Lett's mother stayed at the White Lion Hotel in Hadleigh when she visited as I think she found Benton End rather too chaotic for her liking. Once when Lett exasperated her she said, 'Lett, your father was a fool and you are a fool!' after which I ferried her back to her hotel.

Patrick Ogilvie, a Royal Air Force pilot and Lett's nephew, was a war-time visitor. He would boost Cedric's confidence by assuring him that we would win the war and he need not bury his paintings in the garden. Another good friend who came to Benton End after war service was Nigel Scott, a charming and delightful man. As gardener and plantsman he worked with Cedric in the large garden and together they made many trips abroad looking for new plants. Sadly Nigel died while they were abroad. Beth Chatto was a frequent visitor and good friend. She propagated some miniature daffodil bulbs which Cedric had brought back from his travels. Every year the garden was opened for the benefit of the British Red Cross. There was great excitement the year that Cedric won an award at Chelsea for the first pink iris to be bred in this country, later named 'Edward of Windsor'†. I was very much involved in reproducing the flower books of two other artist friends of Cedric, Dickie Chopping and John Nash.

There were trips in the black Ford to The Marquis of Cornwallis in Layham …

Summer afternoons were spent in the garden with Lucy (Harwood) taking charge and keeping order at tea-time. Lett shouting to us from his bedroom window added to the fun. While helping Lett prepare the evening meal we would discuss many topics, painting, colour, style and local village gossip, with Lett's earthy comments, and there were trips in the black Ford to The Marquis of Cornwallis in Layham and The King's Arms in Hadleigh to play darts and drink. There was no breathalyser then. There were parties given by Lucy at Kiln House and Lorna Styles at The Pound, a tradition carried on by Tommy and Elizabeth when they lived there.

† According to the records of The British Iris Society this iris was named 'Edward Windsor' and was registered to Sir Cedric Morris in 1945. There is no record of an award being given at that time but in 1949 at the Iris Show the Pesel Challenge Bowl was awarded to Cedric for nine varieties of iris which may have included 'Edward Windsor'.

Lett Haines: *Composition*, 1921. Mixed media. 47 x 60 cm. Private collection.

As the years passed life became quieter at Benton End, but I continued to take my painting for Cedric's opinion and a bottle of wine for Lett. Conversation at the table kept to its usual high standard with Lett's rumbustious humour and Cedric's sharp observations. Visiting Cedric in hospital during his last illness helped to ease the sadness of the ending of a long and happy friendship. Cedric, Lett and all that Benton End meant gave me a lifetime's love of art and painting which widened the horizons of a quiet country boy.

Ellis Carpenter

Ellis Carpenter was born in King's Lynn but was brought up by foster parents in Benton Street, Hadleigh. He became a 'Saturday pupil' at Benton End. His career was in insurance in London. He is a keen painter and has exhibited with Hampstead Outdoor Artists and at Colchester Castle, The Minories, Bury St Edmunds' Art Gallery and the Llewellyn Alexander Gallery, London. Ellis Carpenter breeds and exhibits irises.

Derek Waters first took me to Benton End and introduced me to Lett. After that I went there (and to Lucy Harwood's in Layham) on Saturdays and in the evenings to help in the gardens. Cedric was extremely meticulous about the weeding and did not easily trust his helpers not to pull up plants with the weeds, so at first I worked alongside him, hence my interest in irises. I also helped to maintain Lett's Ford 8 car. When Cedric and Lett went off abroad I was instructed to look after the car and keep an eye on the garden.

Going through the gates of Benton End was like arriving in France. There was a Bohemian atmosphere – the wine, the food and the marvellous conversation. I admired what seemed to me to be a relaxed way of life there, an oasis of calm from everyday life elsewhere.

After National Service I returned to Benton End in 1948, wanting

to paint seriously, (although my foster mother, who was deeply religious, thought all artists were wicked). Lett gave me a palette and taught me the technique of stretching canvases and Cedric gave me some brushes and the recipe for priming my canvases and then they let me get on with developing my own style and technique. I have painted ever since, attending Benton End as a student regularly until 1954, and again from early 1960 every year until Cedric's death.

Lett was a rascal, a dreadful social climber but full of fun. It was he who gave me the nickname of Mayor of Toytown and when I took Tom and Body (Tom and Elizabeth Wright) to the Pound on their wedding day, I received a call from him, 'It's time the Mayor of Toytown returned my car.'

Cedric was quiet and laid back. They were like an old married couple arguing gently. Lett would tease Cedric and Cedric would get annoyed, put his head on one side and his hands on his hips and say, 'Well, we will have to agree to disagree.' Once I was working in the classroom and a camera crew came in to take photographs of Cedric, who was dressed up for the occasion. I did a quick pastel drawing of him while he was posing but he was furious and snubbed me all day. I was later told that nobody was allowed to draw him. When I apologised he made me promise not to develop the drawing into a proper piece of work. I have to confess that another time when he was leaning against a tree arguing with Lett I did a drawing of both of them. However, in the summer of '79, a few months before his ninetieth birthday, a group of ladies from the British Iris Society asked if they could take a photograph of him in the garden. He responded by posing, hands on hips and a big smile on his face. He turned to me and said, 'Now's your chance!' I took it and later finished a portrait in oils.

Once I had to take a phone call from Isaiah Berlin, a great admirer of Cedric, who wanted to give him Christmas greetings. Cedric was a bit embarrassed and very reluctant to speak to him.

Lett introduced another pupil to me as 'Miss Knickerless', referring

Cedric Morris: *Paysage du Jardin*, 1931. Oil on canvas. 70 x 63.5 cm. Private collection.

to the time when she had come to stay bringing only one pair of knickers which she had to wash each night. Cedric said, when she was painting in the garden, 'See what this young woman is doing. Go and get your easel and see what you can do in comparison.' He also told me to look at Lucy Harwood's work and learn from it. Kathleen Hale was a warm person with enormous joy of life, forever poking fun, rather like Lett. Yet she was totally absorbed and serious in her work.

One evening when we were chatting round the bonfire and Bryan Brooke was playing the guitar, two figures in penguin suits loomed up out of the darkness. Cedric exclaimed, 'Good gracious, ghosts out of the fog'. It was Benjamin Britten and Peter Pears who had been dining with Randolph Churchill and had called in on the way home. Britten strummed the guitar and Pears sang 'The foggy, foggy dew'. Not all visitors were so welcome though. When ladies from the British Iris Society arrived Cedric would mutter,' Here come the ducks again.' And on one occasion when Francis Bacon turned up, Cedric said, 'Tell him I am out,' and fled to the top of the garden. We had to help Bacon turn his car round as he was quite unable to manage by himself and just missed the gate as he drove off.

Cedric said, 'Tell him I am out', and fled to the top of the garden ...

I remember that once after Lett had died the fishmonger and the gardener both came for their money. Millie was out shopping and Cedric, of course never had any money, so I paid. When Millie returned she had spent out, so Cedric suggested that I kept Lett's pastels which he had allowed me to use, in lieu of the money. As Cedric grew older I would help him again in the garden, mainly trying to rid the irises of the masses of grass growing in them. Cedric said that I was 'a good friend' and asked me to choose a painting for myself. I chose *Footpath to Alder Carr, 1935*, which added to a small collection of silverpoint drawings which had been used as illustrations for a book of herbs, and another of Cedric's oils entitled *Red Campanula* which was painted on St Helena.

Cedric remains the mentor of my painting and it was his gifts of iris seedlings which started me off with iris breeding.

Kathleen Hale

The late Kathleen Hale studied art at Manchester School of Art and Reading University College. In 1917 she went to London with the ambition to be an artist and to become a part of artistic London life. Her numerous friends included Jacob Epstein and his circle. She was secretary to Augustus John and became close friends with him and his wife, Dorelia. Kathleen Hale worked in the Ministry of Food and the Land Army during World War I. She fulfilled many commissions as an artist and illustrator and designed a ballet for the Festival of Britain celebrations. Kathleen Hale was the creator of the popular Orlando the Marmalade Cat *books for children.*

I first got to know Cedric and Lett in Paris in 1922. After that I saw them intermittently until their deaths. Certainly I accompanied them on the move from The Pound in Higham to Benton End and so I was at Benton End from the start. At that time I was painting passionately and learning lithography at Cowells, the printers in Ipswich. Both Cedric and Lett found their way into illustrations in my Orlando books which I was creating while at Benton End.

The experience that I had at Benton End certainly influenced my development as an artist. I was determined to work in my own way.

Cedric and Lett gave me no praise nor blame, no criticism and no formal instruction. Instead they guided me gently in order that I could find my own direction.

I, like everybody else, recall Cedric and Lett with a lot of affection and great love. Their personalities were unique and different. Both were very open-minded though they were oddly apt to be prejudiced, Cedric particularly. I remember that their somewhat ramshackle, under-furnished house, with no carpets or rugs and in which little housework was done, somehow resulted in a great freedom of mind.

Both were very open-minded though they were oddly apt to be prejudiced . . .

The following extracts are taken from Kathleen Hale's autobiography, A Slender Reputation *reprinted by kind permission of the publishers, Frederick Warne.*

Cedric evolved a science of colours that was venturesome: acid yellow next to shocking pink, scarlet and apple green. He always painted methodically – none of the blood and sweat which most artists go through – without any preliminary drawings. He would begin calmly at the top left hand corner of the canvas and paint down and across until he had completed the whole picture. He never made any corrections, which accounted for the freshness and spontaneity of his painting.

Cedric's tastes were simple; he was almost a puritan, and he never believed in excess, whether in drink – unlike Lett – food, clothes, or entertaining, although he loved parties. He was often prejudiced, especially in politics (he was a passionate left-winger, and deeply concerned about the well-being or otherwise of his beloved Welsh), and was impatient of different points of view, so that to be accepted by him it was necessary to become a sort of disciple.

Cedric and Lett attracted a wide variety of students, established painters as well as eccentric or glamorous people from different worlds. As Cedric was an attractive bachelor, he was a sitting duck for amorous pursuit by middle-aged virgin lady students. 'I'd like to

Lett Haines: *Angry Humble*, 1965. Mixed media. Height 28.7 cm. Private collection.

Kathleen Hale: *Portrait of Lett Haines*. Watercolour. Private collection.

'Lett ... was sophisticated, but could reveal sudden glimpses of child-like innocence.'

shake a wet lettuce up their petticoats,' he would say, and fall into paroxysms of giggles ...

Lett's painting was completely different from Cedric's: low in colour, linear, intellectual, sometimes weird, and sometimes abstract, often erotic. Later in his life, when he and Cedric ran their second school of art in Suffolk, he collected rabbit and chicken bones from the students' meals and constructed extraordinary small 'groups' from them. He called these his 'Humbles'. I remember one especially, a few inches high, which he called 'The Garden': delicate white thigh-bones, densely packed together, rooted in plaster, knobby little joints pointing upwards like buds on stalks, evocative of alien plant forms growing in a cellar. Some of these groups were nightmarish, and one, made only of rough plaster, was a strange, luridly-coloured, curdled mess suggesting blood and mud, topped by a staring human glass eye.

Lett was six feet tall, with a fine physique, and regular features saved from being conventionally good-looking by his slightly satanic eyebrows, piercing grey eyes (which I teased him by likening to pieces of splintered glass), and a mouth he described as resembling a split liver. He went bald in his early twenties, but was inspired to keep his whole head shaved like a Tibetan monk, giving him a distinguished but sometimes sinister air. His personality was composed of many warring factors. He was sophisticated, but could reveal sudden glimpses of child-like innocence. Mischievous and sometimes wicked, he liked to dramatise situations, and delighted in stirring up scandals. He was exceptionally patient and unself-serving, but, though fundamentally affectionate and gentle, his razor-sharp perception of the strengths and weaknesses of the human race made him an adept manipulator, able to detect people's most sensitive areas and to wound them. Like the caddis-fly grub acquiring a carapace of sticks and stones, Lett attracted an entourage of all ages and from varied environments. He is the Katnapper in *Orlando's Silver Wedding:* I based the character's magnetism for cats on Lett's magnetism for people. (As in the book, Lett really did darn a hole in his check tweed jacket with

Kathleen Hale, *Orlando's Silver Wedding*: Lett as the Katnapper.

white wool and then paint on the pattern in water-colour, but the first time he wore it out of doors in the rain, the water-colour was washed out.) …

Cedric and Lett's method of teaching was centred on discovering and developing hidden talent among students of all ages and from any background. They believed in sensitive guidance, understanding, and respect for individuality, without criticism. This resulted in original work of considerable diversity.

Lett really did darn a hole in his check tweed jacket with white wool and then paint on the pattern in water-colour …

Some who longed to enrol but hadn't the money for fees were given

... elderly ladies, hitherto timid water-colourists, could blossom into riotous colour ...

free tuition if they proved to be serious, even if they were without perceptible talent. It was an atmosphere where elderly ladies, hitherto timid water-colourists, could blossom into riotous colour and bold designs. A group of young boys who tried to join just for a lark were only allowed to do so if they agreed to paint and draw seriously and behave themselves. At least two grew up to become bona fide artists and able to work professionally.

Kathleen Hale, *Orlando's Home Life*: Cedric as the dancing master.

Frank Pond

Frank Pond was born in Norwich and has lived and worked there ever since. He was educated at the City of Norwich School where his interest in art was aroused by the art teacher, Mr W. T. Watling, who founded the Norwich Twenty Group in 1944. Frank Pond worked for forty years in local government and retired to resume active painting. He has been involved for several years with the Advice Arcade Gallery Group planning, organising and hanging exhibitions. At the time of writing he is the Chairman of the Norwich Twenty Group. Frank Pond paints and exhibits regularly.

In 1944 Miss Aileen Law, art teacher at the Blyth Grammar School for girls, became a pupil of my father who taught the cello. She quickly became a close friend of the family and invariably stayed to tea after her lesson. She encouraged my latent interest in painting and she soon got me organised with oil colours and canvas. Her interest in contemporary painting also struck a chord in me. She had already started to visit the East Anglian School of Painting and Drawing, and much of Cedric's tuition and opinions was passed straight on to me so I knew much about Cedric, Lett and all the Benton End activities before I went there myself.

Lett Haines: *The Escape*, 1931. Indian ink and watercolour. 52.5 x 65 cm. Private collection.

Aileen Law was a great one for 'organising' people's lives, and by

May 1945 decided I was sufficiently developed to visit Benton End. I travelled from Norwich to Ipswich by train and then by bus to Hadleigh. The door was opened to me by Cedric himself, instantly recognisable by the neckerchief and corduroy trousers, and he took me through to where Bernard Reynolds was working at a painting of irises. Benton End was a revelation to me. Coming at the end of the war after five years of dreary existence, making do with worn-out clothes, absence of light and colour everywhere, suddenly to be in this

Cedric Morris:
Quinces and Nerines,
1963. Oil on canvas.
120 x 170 cm.
Private collection.

world of a garden and house full of irises of incredible colours, cats wandering around, and modern, exciting paintings everywhere – it was beyond belief. The food provided by Lett was another revelation – especially the fruit jelly. He insisted that he just threw in a handful of whatever fruits were in season in the garden, plus, of course, the odd spoonful of cooking sherry, which he consumed at the same time.

There was a Fair in the village on the Monday and we all went down to it in the evening. Several stalls were offering prizes of glass beer mugs for knocking down piles of tins with mops. I produced a hitherto-unknown skill in this, and we returned with nine or ten mugs which were used by students for meal time drinking for several years. Lett always fed the cats at about midnight. He would appear at the back door, bang loudly on a tin tray, calling out in a voice that could have been heard miles away – 'Karzes peaz.' Nobody knew for sure what it meant but anyway the cats understood and half a dozen would come running from the garden and the fields as though they were starving.

Lett always fed the cats at about midnight.

Breakfast was very much a 'help yourself' affair, but the main meal cooked by Lett and served by Cedric was always excellent. The war in Europe had just finished, but food rationing went on for many years. Students had to take ration books with them and Lett would cut out an appropriate number of coupons, but I am sure we all ate well beyond the rationing of the time. Lett consumed a fair amount of wine, and although you never actually saw him drunk, on the other hand you never actually saw him sober. He was a terrific snob, and on one occasion said, 'I have found a student's cap – has anybody lost one?' On being asked how he knew it was a student's cap he replied, 'It is not a Lock's of St James or a Simpson's so it must be a student's.'

I only visited Benton End once or twice after that as the business of earning a living took over from other interests, but the impression it made on me has lasted all my life, and I feel privileged to have shared for a short time the remarkable world of Benton End.

Cedric Morris: *Mixed Flowers*, 1947. Oil on canvas. 46 x 36 cm. Private collection.

Robert Davey

Robert Davey ('Stoner Monk') was a solicitor with practices in Hadleigh and Ipswich and is trustee for both Lett's and Cedric's estates. He was a close friend for many years and a frequent visitor to Benton End.

I was one of the earliest arrivals at Benton End in 1942 as part of a group of local lads mainly from Benton Street: Derek Waters, Ronnie Spraggons, Jack Beckett, Ted Lilley, Maurice Hines and Ellis Carpenter. We viewed Benton End and its occupants with some suspicion, not being sure what went on there. Gradually though, we drifted down there to receive a warm welcome from both Cedric and Lett and spent many happy hours with Cedric in the garden, always looking forward to the morning and afternoon tea sessions.

For my part I became very involved with Benton End, painting not too successfully and doing quite a lot of design work for one of the students, Trevor White, who designed fashionable headscarves. I joined the East Anglian School of Painting and Drawing as its Secretary, though Lett preferred the posher title of Stenographer. The job covered a multitude of sins; I attended students with their luggage, looked after the bookings, sold art materials, made canvases with hessian sugar bags when canvas was difficult to come by and even assisted Lett with the cooking and washing-up. I also dealt with the suppliers, all local shops except Spearing of Dedham.

I remember Cedric's various commissions of bird and flower paintings for Shell and Toucan adverts for Guinness. Once he went to Southampton to the *Queen Mary* to repair one of his paintings which had been boarded up while the vessel was used as a troopship during the war. Of course Cedric's special pleasure was his garden where he produced many new varieties of iris. He was very well known and respected in the horticultural world.

Some three hundred yards down the road from Benton End stood a row of cottages known as Rubbish Row which were destroyed by fire in the nineteen-forties. Cedric and Lett had no hesitation in taking in the homeless families and giving them food and shelter until they were re-housed.

Nearly all the students who attended Benton End were given a *nom de plume* by Lett which was promptly produced from poster advertising lettering and stuck on the wall of the 'little room' on the ground floor for all to see. Mine was Stoner Monk.

Nearly all the students were given a nom de plume *by Lett …*

My own association with Benton End was a very happy one and I shall always be grateful to Lett and Cedric for my original grounding in a wide scope of topics which I am sure stood me in good stead during my working career. I also met many interesting people over the years like Bobbie and Natalie Bevan, David and Barbara Carr, Boo Boo Banbury, Dr Bob Smith, John Nash, Kathleen Hale (Moggie), Henley Curl and Lucy Harwood.

Benton End was unique.

Bernard Brown

Bernard Brown left Hadleigh in 1956 for National Service in the so-called Malayan Emergency. Suspecting he might be on the wrong side, he sought and gained a local discharge and became a law lecturer at Singapore University. After three years he was moved out and on to New Zealand. In 1966 he became Foundation Fellow in Papua New Guinea Law, where jurisprudence took third place to survival and anthropology. Four years later he resumed his law teaching at Auckland University, New Zealand. Recently he was made an officer of the New Zealand Order of Merit. Regularly over the past forty years he has returned to Hadleigh where his mother has resided. Among Bernard's publications are four volumes of poetry, two of which he has illustrated.

Until my father arrived in the early 1930s there was no Labour Party branch in Hadleigh. A man of scant formal education himself, he was nevertheless determined that the locals saw something of thinkers like Arthur Greenwood and John Platts Mills. I suspect that Dad made overtures to Cedric and Lett in the late 1930s because it was then that he lured Professor Catlin, political philosopher and Shirley Williams' father, to The Marquis of Cornwallis, their favoured

... the ambience of Benton End was deliciously exotic.

Cedric Morris: *Crisis*, 1939. Oil on canvas. 122 x 91 cm. Private collection.

watering hole. A decent-sized audience stood outside the pub to listen and debate. It was later rumoured that at the 1945 General Election Cedric and others from Benton End ambushed with bad eggs the sitting member, a disagreeable Tory named Colonel Burton. Dad was a magistrate by this time so would have been present in spirit only.

In about 1940 my parents decided to send me to Benton End 'to draw'. Other local boys included Derek Waters, Robert Davey ('Stoner') and Ellis Carpenter. Tommy Wright was already part of the artistic establishment. Starting somewhat later was a girl from George Street, Maggi Hambling. Certainly I was attending there when German bombers were passing overhead to and from London and the Hook of Holland. My mother was concerned that I was out at such times as there had been a few stray bombs on Hadleigh and she entreated me to stay at home. Not a hope! To a seven- or eight-year-old village lad the ambience of Benton End was deliciously exotic. 'Camp' had more than the tented meaning. Besides Lett and Cedric there were Millie and Hetty. Lucy Harwood, residing in Layham, was a regular. A statuesque model from Raydon posed at some life classes. A good, traditional, full-figure nude of her hung for decades in the big room by the front entrance. The early war years brought us one or two male models from London, 'conchies', it was rumoured. My father became anxious about my drawing naked men but Cedric sorted that out. I gloried in Lett's *double entendres* and remember particularly a sustained series of them – inspired whimsy – concerning Sonja Henie, the comely film star ice-skater who had alleged that a Nazi admirer had molested her. Lett's verbal gymnastics must have increased my interest in language. Indeed the first poem I published, decades later, in *The Australian* in 1967, was vintage Lett. It nearly cost me my job!

A person who caught my eye was a once-only visitor in her seventies, Frances Hodgkins. Cedric had taken her under his wing in his Chelsea days. I was told she was 'the New Zealand lady' who had

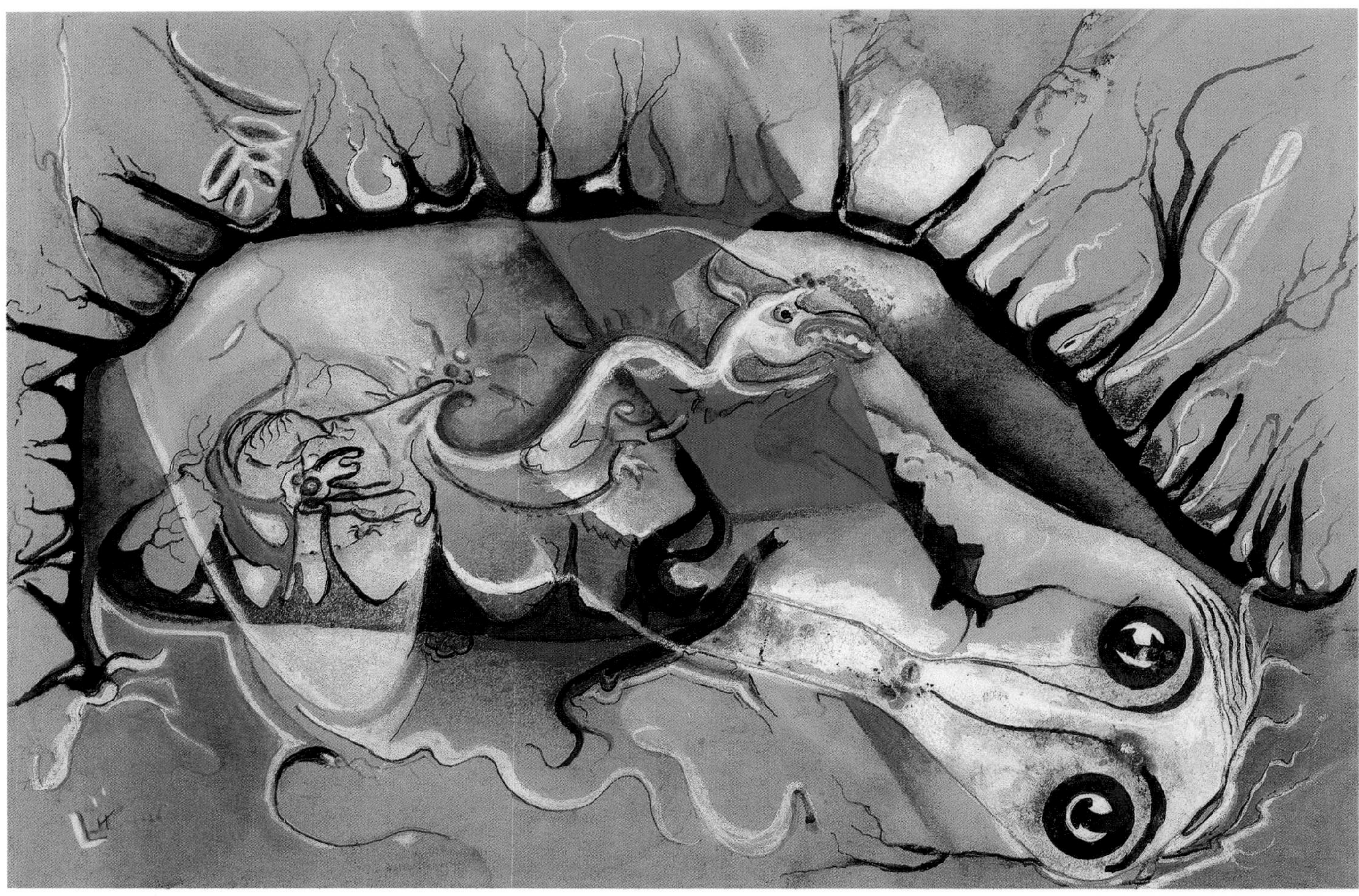

Lett Haines: *Poor dolly*, 1966. Mixed media and collage. Height 25 cm. Private collection.

been unwell. I was requested to go to the river across the road and get clay for her to work on a potter's wheel. She wasn't good at it. Much later I learned she was ranked highly among mid-twentieth-century English painters. A painter's painter. In 1962 I met in New Zealand the belletrist, Dr Eric McCormick, who had written a biography of

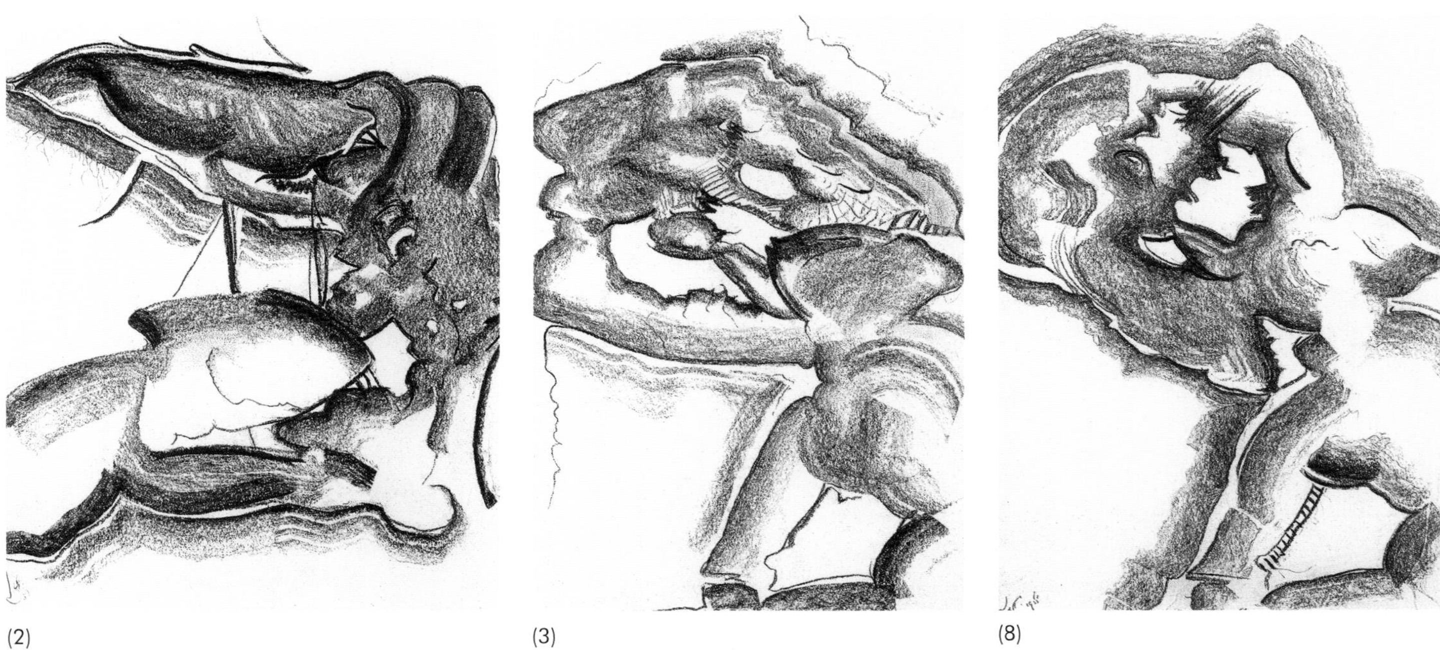

(2) (3) (8)

Lett Haines: *Studies for Dragon's Mate*, 1955.
(2) Black conte. 29 x 23 cm.
(3) Black conte. 35 x 24 cm.
(8) Black conte. 32.5 x 23 cm.
Private collection.

Frances Hodgkins called *The Exile*. Eric had visited Hadleigh ten years before. He stoked a revival of Australasian interest in Hodgkins and acknowledged the practical and spiritual support Cedric had given her. Cedric's portrait of her hangs in the Auckland City Gallery. When I visit it I hear again Cedric telling me to fetch some clay for her. It was said sadly, for he knew age and illness were beginning to take their toll of her painting talent.

Nigel Scott I remember well, notably when he walked nightly with Cedric and others to the Marquis of Cornwallis or to The Monkey (The King's Arms) in Benton Street. Lucian Freud always created a stir and the Pipers visited several times during my sojourn. Derek Waters told me there were psychiatrists from London too. Psychotherapists, more likely. Some kind of aesthetic link between them and artists was forged in the 1920s and '30s and they may have had some influence on Dada and Surrealism.

The food at Benton End was aromatic and plentiful, despite rationing, and Lett would hold court at table. Meals were times for unwinding and mock insults would be traded. The gardener, Arthur Girling, a World War I veteran, would shake his head and rattle on to me about the weirdness of the 'arty-crafty' gentry. Girling, who had been commissioned in the trenches in 1917 when all around him were falling, and took the war very seriously, regularly exhorted the Benton Enders to comply with blackout regulations which they did not always do. In the early years of World War II, Hadleigh-ites were stewing in the moral panic of The Hostilities and lost no chance to be cruel to any locals with German connections. In that atmosphere two plus two often equalled five. The bombing of the old Tinkers Lane Mill was even linked by local gossip to one of Cedric's guests having painted it some months earlier. (Presumably the oil painting was shipped to Luftwaffe HQ and then hung in the cabin of a Dornier which scoured the Suffolk countryside trying to spot the strategic target!) Cedric and his friends soon complied with blackout restrictions and, although some conscientious objectors continued visiting Benton End, there was no more open or covert antagonism. Nevertheless, for years after the war, people still thought that Lett, who sported what looked like a sabre scar on his pate, was a former Prussian cavalry officer. He was probably rather more English than they were! No one seemed to know that Cedric and Lett had had 'good wars' for Britannia thirty years before.

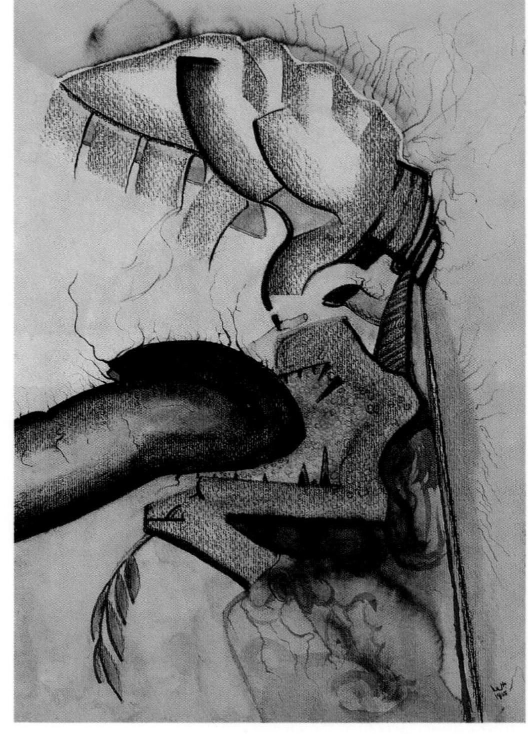

Lett Haines: *The Martyrdom of Purple Hampton*, 1955. Mixed media. 36 x 25 cm. Private collection.

A Benton End project that arose out of the war years was the design and painting of new Hadleigh and district pub signs. These had been dismantled in 1939 in case the enemy invaded and found them geographically helpful. After VE Day, Cedric and Tommy Wright thought it timely to paint really imaginative signs and re-hang them, but only a few were done and, to my knowledge, only

Tommy's, of the Hadleigh Shoulder of Mutton, was displayed by the brewery.

My father retained a link with Cedric right up to the latter's death, through the Labour Party. Whenever I was home on leave from Singapore, New Guinea or New Zealand I was encouraged to visit 'Sir Cedric'. I did so on several occasions and found he was more intrigued with my travels (I had been shot by an arrow on my way up the Sepik River!) than with my law career or the little painting I did. With the latter I had had two bits of success as a schoolboy. In the early '40s I won a BBC Children's Hour self-portrait competition ('The Picture of Dorian Brown' according to Lett), and at the age of sixteen or seventeen a couple of my paintings had been finalists in the Sunday Pictorial schools art contest. They were execrable and I didn't dare show them at Benton End. Come to think of it, nothing about technique was ever taught me there. Occasionally someone might say 'good' or 'dreadful', but we were left to our own devices, thank goodness.

... Lett and Cedric sometimes went months without speaking to each other ...

It began to dawn on me that all men were not alike and I did wonder why Lett and Cedric sometimes went months without speaking to each other but assumed it was part of being 'bohemian'. There were risqué jokes posted in the big lavatory, where words had been excised from Hadleigh cinema programmes and juxtaposed to make sexual puns. Obviously there was more argument, self-questioning and more openness than a country boy's home-life accommodated. Benton End must have been magnetic to me because despite being a 'swot' and a sport addict, I kept going back to Cedric and Lett. What I derived from 'the artists' was a further, and richer, metaphorical dimension to a routine, if nosey, childhood.

Millie Hayes

The late Millie Hayes was the mainstay of Benton End for many years, from 1964 until Cedric's death. Her cooking was legendary. She lived in Hadleigh, Suffolk.

I first met Cedric in London, in Percy Street in Mrs Beulah's café where I would go for coffee and a croissant and to read the newspapers from all over the world. Artists used to gather there and at Bertorelli's in the area round Charlotte Street. I modelled for a portrait by Cedric, though not in the nude! I was a writer at the time, having done well at school, Malvern Girls' College, and though I was under twenty-one I was very independent.

I first went to Benton End for a week's holiday to paint. I remember that Lett and Glyn Morgan were painting in the studio upstairs. Cedric was abroad. He and Lett used to get so incensed with one another that they would go separately for their holidays. When Cedric was away, Lett would manage everything by himself, trying to fit in his painting between his cooking, so I offered to come and cook for them and in 1964 I came to live at Benton End and stayed there until Cedric's death.

Before then I had worked in the Elephant Hotel in Pangbourne as a stillroom maid, doing all sorts of jobs such as washing-up, typing and cooking, so the old Aga at Benton End, which no-one wanted when Cedric and Lett tried to throw it out, held no difficulties for me.

Cedric Morris: *Wood Pigeons*, 1929. Oil on canvas. 62.5 x 76 cm. Private collection.

Cedric Morris: *Irises Heralding*, 1959. Oil on canvas. 72.5 x 97.5 cm. Private collection.

Peter Wakefield

Sir Peter Wakefield was a friend and fellow student of Gerry Stewart, Lett-Haines's nephew. Sir Peter's career was in the army and in the diplomatic service. He is the Chairman of Asia House and the former director of the National Art Collections Fund.

I had come from a rather narrow background and had attended a conventional public school and spent some years in the army so I had not encountered anything like Benton End before. Its atmosphere attracted me enormously. Cedric and Lett made an art out of living which was open, fun and life-enhancing.

Lett was interested in people and could notice things which one might have preferred to remain unseen and unsaid. He had an essential grasp of the importance of art, and all those who shared this were welcome. He had wide intellectual interests and was generously supportive to those who needed his help. Lett tended to be excessively impressed by my position in the diplomatic service. He had an amusing habit of exaggerating my status as a 'diplomatist', so when only a humble First Secretary, I became his friend the Counsellor, and when a Counsellor I was referred to as his friend the Ambassador. It made it all more fun.

Cedric I admired for his puckish charm, his beautiful garden and, of course, his painting. His absolute concentration on his personal vision was impressive. I rushed to Benton End as soon as I came home on leave to see and hopefully to capture one of Cedric's paintings. Our house is filled with his joyful pictures and our children share our pleasure and love of them.

I suppose I had always been blessed with an eye to see but I had been brought up to suppress my love for 'pretty' things as if it was something unmanly, to be ashamed of. Benton End offered me the encouragement to sanction my love for paintings and sculpture. The experience of Benton End gave me an abiding interest in art which led me eventually to become director of the National Art Collections Fund. My present work as Chairman of the Asia House gives me the opportunity to encourage the performance and exhibition of Asian arts in this country. Benton End indeed changed my life.

I rushed to Benton End as soon as I came home on leave …

Lett Haines: *The Lion Hunt*, 1929. Watercolour and pastel. 46 x 62 cm. Private collection.

Felicity Wakefield

Felicity Wakefield is the daughter of Rose Marrable who went to Benton End at the end of the World War II. Felicity had her first holiday at Benton End in 1947. She and her husband Peter, whom she married in 1951, were frequent visitors until Cedric's death. Lett and Cedric often stayed with the Wakefields in London and Cedric once paid them a two-month visit when they were living in Libya, during which he painted and collected plants.

I first came to Benton End with my mother who often stayed there and who at one time, shortly after the war, undertook the housekeeping for Lett and Cedric. My mother would not allow me to go to art school to learn sculpture as I wished. She thought that I should earn my living more profitably. Cedric dug up some clay for me from the river below the garden and I modelled a ceramic head, the first of many.

From the beginning I found Lett warm and affectionate and I loved him. He was a disconcerting person and Cedric used to say of him that he could say things which hurt people. He had an intellectual understanding of art and was a superb critic.

Peter and I went to Benton End during our honeymoon when Cedric presented us with a picture of two doves, saying, 'I wondered what to give you for your wedding.' We became great friends with Lett and Cedric who often stayed with us in London and abroad. When we visited them we used to drive Cedric about to see his friends. There was a Jaguar in the garage which Lett dreamed about driving, though he never did.

Over the years we bought many paintings, and I believe we have the first picture Cedric ever painted and the last, an unfinished but beautiful study of succulents. Cedric painted my portrait. It was intended to be of both of us, but Peter fidgeted so much during the sittings that Cedric in despair cut the canvas in half, leaving Peter out.

Cedric Morris: *Café Scene*, 1920.

Michael Chase

The late Michael Chase was Director of the Zwemmer Gallery, London, from 1954 to 1965 and The Minories, Colchester, from 1966 to 1974. At one time he was Honorary Director of the Digby Gallery at the Mercury Theatre in Colchester, an Honorary member of Colchester Art Society and a Trustee of Harlow Art Trust. Michael Chase was a water colourist who exhibited frequently in East Anglia and London. His work is represented in a number of private and public collections and is featured in several publications. In 1986 he was the recipient of the Barcham Green Co. award for outstanding watercolour on the company's paper at an Open Exhibition of British Watercolours at Bankside Gallery.

My first contact with Cedric Morris was in December 1965 when he came to the private view of an exhibition at the Zwemmer Gallery in London. I ran this innovative gallery between 1954 and 1965. In pre-war days it had introduced artists like Picasso to England and working there brought me into contact with many of the most important artists of the day. I opened a new room in the basement for printmakers and Valerie Thornton, who was later to become my wife, was one of the exhibitors. She had visited Benton End several times, but even so, it was a lovely surprise to see Cedric, who hated London, come to see her prints. When we

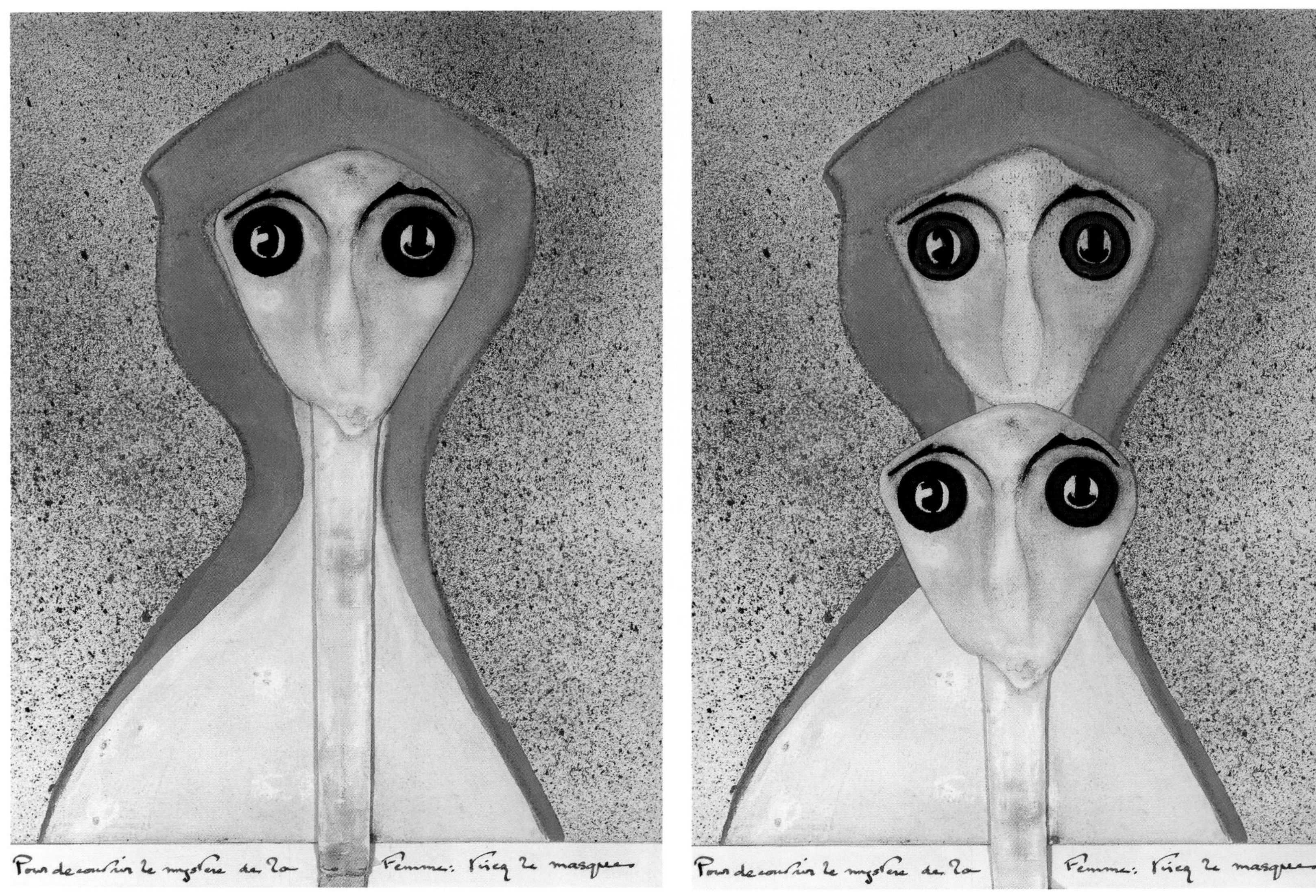
Pour decouvrir le mystere de la Femme: Tirez le masque
Pour decouvrir le mystere de la Femme: Tirez le masque

were introduced, I happened to mention my desire to leave London and he suggested that I should apply for the post of curator at The Minories in Colchester. I did so and got the job – I certainly had the kind of contacts that were needed – and in January 1966 Valerie and I started living in The Minories. But for Cedric, I would not be in East Anglia now.

After that I went to Benton End regularly and I met the 'Benton Enders' like Joan O'Malley (née Warburton), known as Maudie, and Bryan Brooke. I got involved with the Colchester Art Society – Cedric was on the committee too. I mounted exhibitions at The Minories of Lett-Haines' and Bryan Brooke's work and, together with Richard Morphet, worked on the retrospective of Cedric Morris at the Tate in 1984. As a result of all this, Cedric made me his Art Executor.

He had a special quality – a love for people and a tremendous sense of humour.

There was a very special atmosphere about Benton End. Both Lett and Cedric were brilliant hosts and conversationalists and famous people from all over the world came because of the unconventional nature of the school. People treasured all their lives the experience of being students there. Lett and Cedric would give a certain amount of advice but it was all very free and easy. The evenings were the thing, when everybody sat round the table in the kitchen. Lett particularly was a wonderful raconteur. He had a special quality – a love for people and a tremendous sense of humour. He was a wicked man in a way and he certainly had a great liking for society ladies, but I had a great affection for him. His work was marvellous but he did very little because his time was taken up with organising the school and the kitchen. He and Cedric had their differences. He would say of Cedric, 'He's in that bloody garden', and Cedric would say, 'The nigger in the woodpile is a certain Arthur Lett-Haines.'

My job at The Minories was absolutely full time, making introductions, arranging and hanging exhibitions and I was never one of the students at Benton End, though I had always painted in my own individual way. Cedric once said of one of my paintings, 'It is better than I'd dared hope!'

Lett Haines: *Pour decouvrir le mystere de la Femme, tirez le masque*, 1966. Mechanical mixed media. 30 x 22.5 cm. Private collection.

Beth Chatto

Beth Chatto has created and run the Beth Chatto Gardens and Nursery at Elmstead Market near Colchester since the 1960s. She was a founder member of Colchester Flower Club. Influenced by her husband's life-long research into the natural homes of garden plants, she emphasises in her writing the need to find the right plant for the right place. A recent publication is The Gravel Garden *based on a horticultural experiment, where in a three-quarter acre of poor gravel soil, with an average annual rainfall of twenty inches, she has since 1992 grown plants adapted to drought, without irrigation, hoping it may help gardeners who have hose-pipe bans.*

It must have been sometime during the mid 1950s when I met Cedric Morris through a dear friend, Nigel Scott. The garden at Benton End on good loamy soil was a cornucopia with a wealth of bulbs and herbaceous plants I had not seen before. Cedric grew predominantly species plants not generally grown in English gardens at that time.

Cedric was not primarily a plant collector, though when he travelled abroad to paint, he also brought back seeds for his garden. He was, however, one of a circle of plantsmen who travelled to each others' gardens and exchanged plants.

Cedric Morris: *Succulents in Schnake's Pot*, 1969. Oil on canvas. 115 x 94 cm. Private collection.

Cedric had an eye for the structure and form of plants and strong ideas about the tones of colour he preferred. Although he had enough scientific knowledge to breed irises and was indeed the first to breed a pink iris, he was no showman and rarely exhibited his plants at shows. When American imports with their brighter, less subtle colours arrived in the country Cedric preferred to drop out of the race.

Gardening is an artificial concept but needs to be guided by nature. My own gardening is based on detailed consideration of the ecological conditions in which plants can best flourish. Once, when Cedric and I were looking at my garden, I made the comment that we were none of us doing anything new, but Cedric replied, 'We may have the same palette but we are all creating a different picture'. My husband's research has influenced my garden design but it was Cedric Morris who provided me with much of the colour, texture and form on my palette.

The following article entitled 'Sir Cedric Morris, Artist–Gardener' is from By Pen & by Spade, *an anthology from* Hortus: A Gardening Journal *No. 1 Spring 1987, reprinted here by kind permission of the editor.*

'We may have the same palette but we are all creating a different picture'.

I first met Cedric Morris about thirty-five years ago, when I was half his age, and he was the age I am now. This is how it came about. Staying with us one summer weekend was a family friend, Nigel Scott, an impulsive, exciting person, gifted with a charm that made him friends wherever he went. He was also an enthusiastic plantsman. He did not know Cedric, but knew of his famous garden. Why shouldn't we go over and see it? It would not have occurred to Andrew and me to invite ourselves, but Nigel had no such qualms. He rang Benton End, and off we went, winding through narrow Suffolk lanes between drifts of Queen Anne's lace, innocent of what lay ahead, unaware that this day was a turning point in the lives of us all.

We arrived, walked across the gravel yard, knocked at the old wooden door and entered a large barn of a room, the like of which we

Bunches of drying herbs and ropes of garlic hung from hooks on a door …

had never seen before. Pale pink-washed walls rising high above us were hung with dramatic paintings of birds, landscapes, flowers and vegetables whose colours, textures and shapes hit me as though I were seeing them all for the first time. Bunches of drying herbs and ropes of garlic hung from hooks on a door, while shelves were crammed with coloured glass, vases, jugs, plates with mottoes – a curious hotch-potch, remnants from travels in years past. Filling the centre of the room was a long, well-scrubbed refectory table, and round it a rim of heads turned towards us. From the far end of the table a tall lean figure rose immediately, hand outstretched, informal and courteous. This was Sir Cedric Morris, artist and famous gardener, elegant in crumpled corduroys, a soft silk scarf around his long neck upon which was a fine head crowned with short-cut waving hair. His tanned face creased into a mischievous grin. Without fuss, a space was made, chairs were shuffled round on the bare yellow brick floor, three more mugs were found, Cedric poured tea and the conversation resumed. I took a deep breath and listened, feeling incapable of any worthwhile contribution. I was the wife of Andrew Chatto, fruit farmer and grandson of a publisher. Andrew's real interest and life-long study was finding the origins and natural associations of garden plants so that we might know better how to grow them. I was also the mother of two small daughters: much of my time was spent teaching myself the art and crafts of home-making. I was already influenced by Andrew to appreciate species plants as well as cultivars, but my knowledge was much more limited than Andrew's who knew and recognised plants through his studies.

Tea finished, the party broke up. Nigel, Andrew and I were invited into the garden. It was not a conventionally designed garden with carefully selected groups of trees and shrubs leading the eye to some premeditated feature or walk. There were surprisingly few trees or shrubs. Before Cedric's time it was probably a kitchen garden, and was surrounded by still sound brick walls, the enclosed area divided into rectangles by straight and narrow paths. Low box hedges had been planted along the path edges. Some years later I was pleased to

see these disappear and better use made of the space and time required to keep the box in good condition. A few ancient fruit trees were dotted around. Among them a tall cherry made the principal feature, wreathed with ropes of wisteria; sadly, it all collapsed one night in a wild storm. The other remarkable feature was a vast, spreading medlar (*Mespilus germanica*) whose umbrella-like head covered a wide area, valued by Cedric for those precious plants requiring shade and shelter from the drying winds.

You may look, but you will not see without knowledge to direct your mind.

Dotted here and there were pillars of old-fashioned roses and several huge clumps of sword-leafed *Yucca gloriosa*. The rest was a bewildering, mind-stretching, eye-widening canvas of colour, texture and shapes, created primarily with bulbous and herbaceous plants. Later I came to realise it was probably the finest collection of such plants in the country. But that first afternoon there were far too many unknown plants for me to see, let alone recognise. You may look, but you will not see, without knowledge to direct your mind. As you become familiar with more plants and plant families your eye will pick out the unfamiliar ones and so add to your pleasure and knowledge. Walking behind the three men, pricking up my ears (I knew perhaps one Latin name in ten) I felt like a child in a sweet shop, wanting everything I saw. Ecstatic, I knew I must grow such plants in my own garden.

It is no exaggeration to say that at Benton End not only the plants, but the people too were 'characters'. Larger, more intimidating, more intriguing than any, was Arthur Lett-Haines, always called Lett. An inventive, introspective painter, he and Cedric had lived together since the end of the First World War. He ran the household. I doubt if Cedric could boil an egg; he rarely wrote a letter. Lett organised and taught in the East Anglian School of Painting and Drawing, which he and Cedric founded, and of which Cedric was principal. He practically gave up his own work during the latter years of his life to foster Cedric's talents and promote his work. He cooked for the students, who were of all ages and from all walks of life, and for numerous visitors, complaining eloquently as he stirred the pot with one hand, a glass of wine in the other, producing at the end of it memorable dishes.

Cedric Morris: *Easter Bouquet*, 1934. Oil on canvas. 64 x 64 cm. Private collection.

Lett introduced me to Elizabeth David's books (the three of them had been friends for many years). He sent me into the garden to find wild strawberries beneath the rose bushes, he showed me how to make salad on a chill March evening with blanched pink and cream leaves of sea kale. But it was Cedric who gave me a little type-written catalogue, produced by Kathleen Hunter, who supplied seed of unusual vegetables long before they appeared, in colour, in much grander catalogues. Most of them were not new; in fact they could all be found in *The Vegetable Garden*, published in 1885, written by Messieurs Vilmorin-Andrieux, of Paris, beautifully illustrated with fine line drawings describing all the different kinds of vegetables and salads grown in the latter half of the nineteenth century when gardeners were expected to know how to provide a wide variety of fresh food for the kitchen all the year round. In a way, my interest in unusual plants began in my kitchen garden. Growing unusual vegetables and salads was good training when eventually I came to organise a tidy nursery.

A few months after that first visit we were not surprised when Nigel went to live at Benton End. He looked like a Viking, with his narrow face, handsome hooked nose and sharply jutting eyebrows. By nature a pacifist, Nigel volunteered to fight in Finland in the last war, arriving there without proper clothing or equipment to deal with the terrible conditions. Eventually he escaped to England via Norway and spent the rest of the war in a minesweeper in the Mediterranean, occasionally being dropped off to spend a few days climbing in the southern Alps, where his interest in species plants began. When peace came he attempted to settle down in a West Country nursery, but he was not equipped for organised routine. The atmosphere at Benton End was, by comparison, relaxed. Nigel added his own aura and fitted into the scheme of things as they were. During his time there the garden expanded and blossomed to the peak of its development and fame. This takes nothing away from Cedric as its creator; in Nigel he found a companion who shared his enthusiasm for plants to its fullest extent. They worked together, often from dawn till dusk.

He was the first person in this country to produce a pink iris.

It was about this time, the early fifties, that Cedric's work as a

... over the span of a long lifetime he collected, preserved and increased a wealth of plants never before seen together in one place.

breeder of bearded iris was at its peak. He was the first person in this country to produce a pink iris. One of these was first shown in 1948, on the Gold Medal stand at Chelsea of Messrs Wallace, then of Tunbridge Wells. It was admired by Queen Elizabeth, now the Queen Mother, and she allowed it to be called 'Strathmore', after her own home. The names of Cedric's irises were usually preceded by Benton. I have an old Wallace catalogue containing Cedric Morris introductions in 1951 and '52 with romantic names like 'Benton Damozel', Benton Ophelia', 'Benton Fandango'. This last-named variety was a plicata type, meaning the pale silk-textured petals were lightly 'stitched' with fine veins, deepening in tone towards the ruffled edges.

On a few rare occasions, when the iris season was at its best, Cedric and Nigel prepared some of the newest varieties to take to one of the Iris Society shows in London. Can you imagine the performance involved for them to arrive with flowers intact? They had no car, so someone would offer to drive them to the station in Ipswich. Cedric would have hated every minute. He loved to have his plants admired and appreciated but he was not competitive and had no time for pot hunters.

It would be a pity if the records show Cedric only as a famous breeder of iris. Those of us who knew him and his garden over the last thirty years cannot adequately express our debt to him for introducing to us such an amazing collection of unusual plants, primarily species plants rather than cultivars. Today the National Council for the Conservation of Plants and Gardens is doing valuable work, with many specific genera being cared for individually in separate gardens. To us, Cedric's garden appeared to contain them all! An exaggeration, perhaps, but over the span of a long lifetime he collected, preserved and increased a wealth of plants never before seen together in one place. It was practically impossible to take him a plant he did not already possess, although it was tempting to try to do so.

One winter evening after dinner, sitting alone at the table with Cedric and Nigel, I was stunned to hear Cedric say I would never make a good garden where we were living, in our first married home.

My heart dropped to the brick floor while my mind struggled to assess what this meant. We had been pouring ourselves into this garden, battling with chalky boulder clay, while I taught myself to propagate plants from the precious screws of paper full of seed, berries or cuttings I had been given by Cedric as well as generous earthy bundles of roots, tubers and bulbs. We were still far away from the ideal we admired in Cedric's garden, where no season was boring, where each time we visited we found fresh plants we had not noticed before. Several years were to pass before circumstances opened our eyes to the inevitability of building a new home and starting a new garden, but the seed had been planted in the dark of that winter night.

Today the great majority of plants established in our garden at White Barn came originally from Benton End. Certain ones in particular bring Cedric vividly to life in my mind: the many kinds of *Allium*, in flower and seed; the lime-green heads of euphorbia, in particular *Euphorbia wulfenii*, which billowed at the base of a deep Suffolk pink wall; fritillaries, large and small, plum-purple, soft chestnut, or pale lemon-yellow, with speckled or netted insides, looking as if they had been flung into sweeps and drifts among other plants whose season was yet to come! 'How do you get so many?', I would ask when I was still cosseting only two of three of these rare bulbs.

'Scatter the seed', he would say. So I did. But I had to learn, as he had done before me, to nurse the young seedlings for some time before they appeared 'like weeds' in my borders. Old fashioned roses, hellebores, old double primroses, and lace-edged primulas; alas I have almost lost those. There could be pages more.

Cedric abominated salmon-pink: 'Knicker pink!', he would snort. But he loved soft, 'off-beat' shades where the pink was sometimes greyed with tiny purple veins. His interest in breeding, never far beneath the surface, led him to produce an oriental poppy far removed from the bright scarlet and crimson of the species. Its flouncing petals were ashen-pink, with a central velvet knob deep in a pool of dark purple-black blotches. We always called it 'Cedric's Pink', but now it has become officially known as *Papaver orientale* 'Cedric Morris'.

Cedric Morris: *The Blue Poppy*, 1932. Oil on canvas. 70 x 63.5 cm. Private collection.

... the great majority of plants established in our garden at White Barn came originally from Benton End.

His interest in breeding ... led him to produce an oriental poppy far removed from the bright scarlet and crimson of the species.

Another poppy which seeded all over the place at Benton End, with magic effect, was Cedric's selection taken from the wild scarlet poppy of the fields. I think he was aiming to get a lavender-coloured poppy; occasionally he succeeded. Translucent, crumpled petals reflected the soft dove-grey of rain clouds, faintly suffused with pink. Others, in shades of pink, were heavily veined with crimson. Or again, shadowed, shell-pink overlapping petals were edged with a thin dark rim.

Recently I was brought a pan crammed with seedlings of these poppies, preserved by Mary Grierson, whose minutely observed paintings I greatly admire. We sat and indulged in nostalgic memories while she told me how much she owed to Cedric and his garden. It was he who set her on her career as a famous botanical illustrator.

It was not always dream-like. Meal times could be electrified by sudden squalls and conflicts, but the roof never fell in. We sat and waited, suffering with our idols, seeing them as human beings, our bonds of shyness shattered by the storm.

Sometimes there were nightmares. Nigel died, suddenly and tragically. Would summer ever be as bright again? Not long after Nigel's death Millie Hayes found refuge at Benton End. Slender as a flower on a stem, with huge dark eyes and expressive hands, she devoted twenty years of her life, helping to run the household, caring for the two handsome, naughty, darling old men who coloured our lives until eventually the light of each was blown out.

Jenny Robinson

Jenny Robinson's friendship with Cedric Morris began after the war when she was living in Chelsworth in Suffolk. She shared with him a great love of gardening and he asked her to be the executor for his plants after his death to ensure that rarities were left in safe hands. Jenny has wide interests including music and her garden in Boxford.

Cedric had started iris breeding before he moved to Benton End and had created a garden at The Pound in Higham. He was, too, already well known as a painter. His oils of scenery and birds were bold and confident. His portraits were uncomfortably penetrating and had a touch of caricature – he could see right through people – and I always felt his flower paintings (usually life-size) were the same: he understood their characters perfectly – hence his success as a gardener! Despite this ability, however, Cedric was innately kind and had a marvellous gift for putting people at their ease. People were not shy for long in his company. Cedric took a very relaxed view of gardening (and everything else!). 'The only rule is that there are no rules', he once said, and I never heard him talk in botanical terms about anything to do with gardening: he just understood the nature of plants and it worked for him.

Unsurprisingly, life at Benton End was informal. One dropped in without warning and was sure of a welcome, usually finding Cedric on his knees in the garden or perhaps asleep in a chair hidden in the

Cedric Morris: *The Blue Poppy* (Detail), see p. 90.

shade, with the odd student at an easel nearby. I was a near neighbour and I had to restrain myself from going too often – he was always such fun. We'd gossip about plants and I invariably came away with armfuls of them.

It was at Benton End that Cedric created his last and greatest garden. In the high season, the walled garden was a dream of colour, although one was never made aware of much planting for deliberate effect. Irises were everywhere, both species and hybrids, and the garden was full of rare plants from all over the world, many collected by Cedric during his travels during the winter. He was a generous disseminator of both his knowledge and his plant discoveries, always giving away plants to enthusiasts. The walled garden had been a vegetable garden during the war and there are several paintings of it, with the geometric lines of the cabbages between neatly clipped little hedges all softened by glimpses of the river and cornfields on the far side of the road.

Latterly, most of the iris trial grounds were laid out on the other side of the garden wall. Here too were the bigger trees and lovely bushes of old roses. During the tragically short time in the early 1950s that Nigel Scott, an able plantsman friend, lived at Benton End and was helping Cedric, Nigel built a largish rock garden there. I still remember the exquisite blue patch of *Corydalis cashmeriana*, a plant notoriously difficult to grow in these parts.

By the end of the war, Cedric was well into iris breeding and his garden held about a thousand new seedlings every year. He thrilled the iris world with his pink iris, 'Edward Windsor'. Admittedly, this feat of breeding had already been achieved a little earlier in America, but 'Edward Windsor' was acknowledged as a masterpiece worldwide, as was his 'Benton Cordelia' of 1953, a milky mauve. The long list of Morris's creations concluded with 'Benton Farewell', the year after his death in 1982. Cedric left the contents of the garden to me. It was his wish that his plants should be distributed all over the country after his death. It took years off my life doing it!

'The only rule is that there are no rules.'

Cedric Morris: *Still Life*, 1957. Oil on canvas. 77 x 104 cm. Private collection.

CEDRIC MORRIS. -57

The house at Benton End was old, interesting and inconvenient. Its hub was the kitchen, still flagged and with a large sink, turned into an ornamental feature with Portuguese tiles. It usually had a blazing fire and there was a large refectory table in the middle where the inmates ate off wooden plates. I believe Lett Haines was a very good cook, but I never ate there! After his death in 1978 Millie Hayes officiated: eccentric but curiously elegant, she had been a pupil/model at the school of painting, but having fallen on hard times, she found refuge in her old haunts twenty years later.

By the time I came to know Cedric soon after the war, the school as such had developed into a residential club for birds of a feather from every stratum of society, and one encountered the same people year after year. There was also a constant stream of visitors from all corners of the gardening world, many of whom went home with some rare trophy for their own gardens. These visitors included Vita Sackville-West and close friend and neighbour, John Nash, while young Beth Chatto was inspired by Cedric's influence.

There was also a constant stream of visitors ... many of whom went home with some rare trophy for their own gardens.

During the last two or three years of his life, Cedric's eyesight failed. There were no complaints but, still good-looking, he spent much time sitting in front of the fire. He died quietly in hospital, and after his death the Tate put on a retrospective exhibition of his work, and there, too, was a sketch by Maggi Hambling, an ex-pupil, of his old head on the pillow and his hand clutching hers. It has haunted me ever since ...

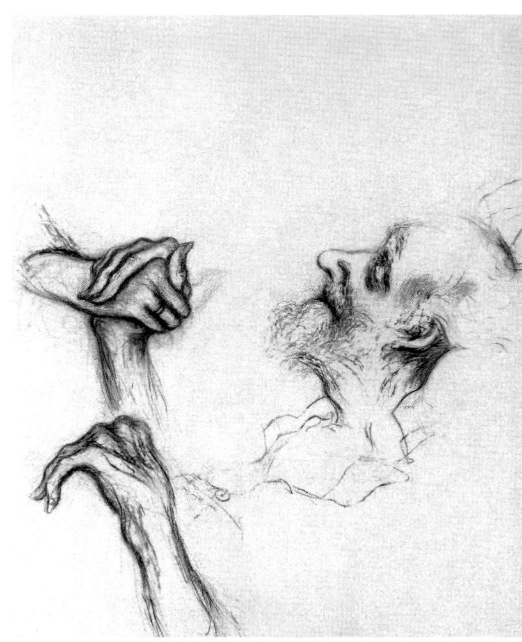

Maggie Hambling: *Cedric, 8th February, 1982.* Charcoal on paper. 76.2 x 55.8 cm. Collection of the artist.

Mostly, when people die, the atmosphere they created gets forgotten too. Not so with Cedric and Benton End. It is extraordinary how many people still remember this atmosphere and the laughing and the kindness. The memorial tablet in Hadleigh cemetery has a plain inscription that says it all:

SIR CEDRIC MORRIS
ARTIST GARDENER
1889–1982

Janet Allen

Janet Allen is a potter who has exhibited in London, Cambridge and Colchester and in her studio in Kettlebaston, Suffolk. She gardens organically, specialising in species plants and in unusual vegetables grown potager-style. She also grows dye plants for dyeing wool and uses ashes from the garden for glazes for her pottery. Janet Allen opens her garden annually to the public in aid of the Henry Doubleday Research Association.

My friendship with Cedric began when I lived in Chelsworth with my young family and spanned about fourteen years. I was introduced to Cedric by my writer friend, Elizabeth Smart, who called me one day to say, 'You must visit this wonderful garden at Benton End'. Her concern was that perhaps Cedric and Lett were moving as the garden fronting the road was so overgrown. When Cedric was told he just laughed and replied, 'I don't garden for the road'. Elizabeth at the time was just starting to create her own unusual garden at The Dell near Bungay in Suffolk.

My friendship with Cedric really began with a mutual love of plants and an offer of weeding. In return for the weeding he gave me seeds, bits and pieces and cuttings, many of which I still have today. I loved his garden; it had such a wild look but was filled with beautiful species plants, a wisteria covering a pear tree and unusual plants collected from his winter travels around the Mediterranean.

Cedric knew so much but was totally modest with his knowledge. The garden attracted many people, not only gardeners but artists and poets too. The legacy of his plants lives on in the Beth Chatto Gardens.

Cedric knew so much but was totally modest with his knowledge.

Cedric Morris: *Golden Auntie*, 1923. Oil on canvas. 65 x 81 cm. Minories.

Fiona Bonny

Fiona Bonny is a primary schoolteacher and self-employed organic market gardener. After taking a degree in History of Art she first cooked in a bistro in Colchester and then, from 1972–75, gardened part-time for Cedric Morris at Benton End. She studied at East Suffolk College of Agriculture and Horticulture before setting up her own market gardening business, initially at Great Horkesley in Essex and now at Boxford, Suffolk, where she grows organic vegetables and keeps sheep and chickens. Fiona Bonny has also worked as a Ranger for Babergh District Council at three wildlife sites, including the old railway line behind Benton End.

I used to help a friend, Janet Allen, with her potting and it was she who introduced me to Cedric. After that I cycled to Benton End from my home in Dedham two or three days a week to work in the garden until Cedric's death four or five years later. Although Cedric was no longer an active gardener he used to tell me stories and the names of plants.

The front garden was overgrown and abandoned and many of the beds in the main garden were choked with weeds but there were still masses of unusual plants, particularly shrubs such as double-flowered

Cedric Morris: *Cacti, Sedums and Succulents*, 1941. Oil on canvas. 62 x 46 cm. Private collection.

My main job was to try to deal with the weeds …

pink brambles. There were some wonderfully-flavoured, aromatic alpine strawberries. I loved the many species roses and have some of the same kinds in my own garden now. My main job was to try to deal with the weeds, though sometimes all I could do was to cut them down. The spectacular iris beds had to be moved periodically too. I grew vegetables for the house, turnips, which were particularly popular, spinach, lettuce and chicory, which was blanched in the cellar. One morning I had the strange task of searching along the gravel path for Cedric's false teeth which he had chucked out of his window along with water from his glass. It took me ages to find them.

Millie was a fantastic cook; she produced marvellous meals for everyone, including all the frequent visitors, and was always very kind to me. The experience of those years, which included plucking my first pheasants and sampling Millie's memorable tapioca pudding flavoured with saffron as well as meeting lots of people who were interested in gardening, undoubtedly broadened my outlook and extended my botanical knowledge.

When Cedric died a lot of people were due to come to the house for the reading of the will and I was asked by one of the executors to jolly up the front entrance where I had tomato plants growing. There wasn't time to do anything much so I planted some lobelia and geraniums among the tomatoes. No doubt this odd mix of plants would have greatly amused Cedric.

After Cedric's death I did a course in horticulture at Otley College and my interest in plants continues today.

Cedric Morris: *Iris, Poppies and Clematis* (Detail), see p. 31.

Frances Mount

Frances Mount worked for several years in the Leicester Galleries, London, where she first came upon the paintings of Cedric Morris and Arthur Lett-Haines. During the sixties she was manageress for Elizabeth David (a friend of Lett-Haines) in her cookery shop. After being introduced to Cedric Morris by Primrose Roper, she then moved to Suffolk, to weed the garden, help set up exhibitions and endeavour, usually unsuccessfully, to keep the flow of visitors to the garden away from him. Frances Mount then worked for Suffolk Herbs before starting her own nursery in Polstead, Suffolk which specialises in hardy geraniums. She shared with Cedric a love of native wild flowers and particularly enjoys lecturing on Suffolk wild flowers and hardy geraniums as well as other gardening subjects.

A friend of mine had mentioned to his godmother that I needed to get away from London because of my sinus trouble and that as I had worked in galleries I got on well with artists. It was through her, Primrose Roper, that I was given an interview in the autumn of 1970 with Cedric Morris for a gardening job at Benton End. The idea was that I would weed the garden and Cedric would teach me how to draw, although it didn't quite work out like that, because I spent all my time in the garden. I started in March 1971 and lived in until September when I moved to Stoke-by-Nayland, though I continued to work at Benton End until the end of August 1978. When I first rang Benton End to arrange for my arrival, Lett answered the phone. He misheard my question, 'Can I bring my cat?' and when I arrived with a cat basket, his face was a picture as he realised that I was not bringing a car. Lett always longed to have a means of escaping to the bright lights.

The irises were moved every four or five years ...

The house was freezing cold in March with no heating on the top floor, but the food was delicious and plentiful and there was always plenty to drink. Lots of interesting people came and went and I found it great fun at first, though I later felt that I was often trying to hold the emotional atmosphere together with Cedric, Lett and Millie, the housekeeper.

I had had a country childhood and had cultivated a tiny London garden, so I had some basic knowledge about plants when I started, but I was not much more than a novice and was allowed to weed only the obvious plants like the cranesbill geraniums of which there was a whole bed in leaf. Everything had to be hand-weeded – the walled garden, with its rare plants, by May when the garden was opened for the Red Cross and the rest by the end of the season. The top of the garden was left fairly wild. The bottom part had been cultivated for vegetables during the war, but then was planted entirely with irises inside the box hedges. The irises were moved every four or five years and new ground had to be prepared for them. The walled garden was a Mediterranean type of garden with light soil on a slope facing south and south-west which was large enough to be able to give the plants plenty of room to flourish just where they were planted. The vertical accent was given by cypresses, juniper, pears and cherries, while *Helleborus, Gagea* and *Corydalis solida* under a lovely old medlar provided the horizontal accent. There were also in the walled garden various *yuccas, Kolkwitzia, Viburnum rhytidophyllum, Sophora, Staphylea* and *Elaeagnus angustifolia*. The walls were covered with ivies, wintersweet, rare *Rosa hemisphaerica*, *Rosa persica* and *Garrya elliptica*.

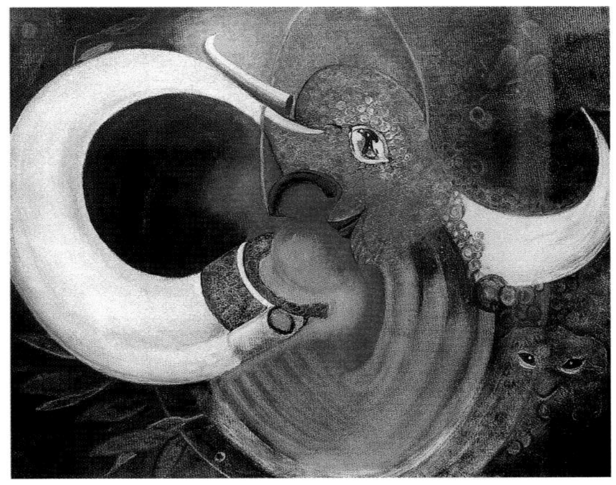

Lett Haines: *Incantation or Sabbat*, 1968. Oil. 49 x 59 cm. Private collection.

Cedric had always travelled extensively, mostly in Europe, during the winter months and had collected seed and bulbs, so there were many rare and unusual plants. There were lots of fritillaries, alliums and small bulbs such as colchicums and cyclamen species. I remember particularly a little narcissus from the borders of Spain and Portugal. There were also species paeonies, tree paeonies – *Paeonia delavayi* and *P. lutea,* rambler roses growing up pear trees, including his own seedling called 'Cedric Morris' and old roses in the grass. Cedric did not go in for shrubs with climbing plants growing through, as is popular today, or for double roses, though he did have one Bourbon rose which he called 'my blowsy lady'. It was very much a painter's garden with much use of strong colours put together, such as orange poppies with scarlet and lots of small plants like old fashioned pinks and dianthus which concentrated the eye. I remember one bed under a pear tree which was beautiful with grey leaves and the dark blue flowers of *Veronica incana* and white *Omphalodes linifolia*. I think that Cedric, who did not express his feelings easily, put his passionate sense of colour into his garden. He was not a botanist and was vague about Latin names but he knew how plants were formed. I think he could not have painted flowers in the way he did without an intimate knowledge of the shape of plants.

It was very much a painter's garden with much use of strong colours put together.

Albert, from Hadleigh, did the mowing and he was also supposed to be in charge of the vegetable garden, though I remember one year when Millie, the housekeeper, and I dug the entire vegetable garden ourselves. Cedric needed help to ward off too many unexpected visitors who prevented him from getting on with his gardening or painting, though when they did appear he would always show them round. As his sight deteriorated, he continued to weed the garden, but it was painful to see him root up rare plants instead of weeds. He was completely unworldly, though practical at tasks like making cement, and he was hopeless at marketing. He had no sense of the commercial value of his plants or pictures. If someone came to buy a picture, Lett would check up on him to ensure that he had been paid or even whether he had money stuffed into his pocket which he had forgotten and I would often help with business and letters. When an exhibition was being prepared, I did a great deal of work cleaning and cataloguing and in return Cedric would give me a picture.

Cedric helped me to realise that I could achieve what I wanted to do. He allowed people to be themselves. He never gave directions or pushed people around. That is why he was so good and unfailingly courteous with amateurs even though he was not particularly fond of them. He influenced my taste in plants and ideas and we shared a love of nature, birds and wildflowers. Even when he was going blind Cedric could identify a bird in flight by its shape.

Cedric helped me to realise that I could achieve what I wanted to do.

Lett, on the other hand, did not like being outdoors. He particularly resented the time Cedric gave to the garden, grudging any time he spent away from his painting. He wanted to absorb people and he still flirted when he was in his eighties. I remember once driving him and Cedric to a party at Wivenhoe and Lett asked me if I remembered the war. He meant World War I and I had to explain that my mother wasn't even born then. On another occasion he said, 'If I were a bit younger I'd have married you.' Lett told Elizabeth David (whom he claimed he had taught how to cook) that if Frances Mount thought that she was going to marry Cedric it would be over his dead body. In the old days they had sometimes had gigantic rows and it was said that at times Cedric had even stomped out and slept in a tent in the garden. Nevertheless, their relationship worked, with Lett cossetting Cedric. Lucy Harwood (who made inedible teas on Sundays) once brought a painting to show Cedric and Lett. Cedric said, 'Less cloud,' while Lett said, 'I like the clouds.' In the end Lucy brought back the painting the next week unchanged.

Later I took a job at Suffolk Herbs, where I did a lot of propagating plants and collecting wildflower seeds and later still I started my nursery. I first became interested in cranesbill geraniums when I weeded them in Cedric's garden long before they became popular

Lett ... did not like being outdoors. He particularly resented the time Cedric gave to the garden ...

Cedric Morris: *Red Wing and Mistle Thrush*, 1928. Oil on canvas. 76 x 64 cm. Private collection.

and I saw what a wide variety of leaf shape, texture and colour they had and how robust they were. Many years after Cedric died I walked round the garden at Benton End with the then owner to find that one of the few plants still surviving among the grass and ground elder was the hardy geranium.

Tony Venison

Tony Venison had his own flower bed by the age of five and has gardened ever since. He managed a nursery for four years before switching to the life of a gardening writer and editor, with more gardening, garden visiting, talking gardening, dreaming gardening and eating gardening – his own vegetables and fruit. Tony Venison was Deputy Editor of Amateur Gardening *and, later, Gardens Editor of* Country Life. *He wrote (with Christopher Neve) an article on Cedric Morris published in* Country Life *in May 1979. He wrote a further article recollecting nine important plants either bred, introduced or found by Morris which was published in* Country Life *on 23 March 2000. Tony Venison now gardens in what he terms half a pocket handkerchief in Suffolk.*

I had known Cedric Morris's plants before I knew Cedric but it was not until 1971 that I knocked on the door and introduced myself as a fellow gardener. After that I was a fairly frequent visitor because, as Cedric used to say, 'It is always such a relief to talk about plants.' Sometimes we didn't speak much because Cedric enjoyed sharing the quietness. Then suddenly he would say something interesting and memorable about plants, places he had been to or about his life.

Cedric Morris: *Still Life before Sussex Fireback*, 1969. Oil on canvas. 78.5 x 96 cm. Minories.

His garden was a wonderful collection of plants, what nowadays might be called an ecological garden, though the term would have infuriated him. It was not tidy in the conventional sense, yet it was orderly in that Cedric knew exactly the whereabouts of each plant. He had a preference for wild plants and could be damning about those man-made plants which he considered had been monkeyed about with too much. Some plants have a poor constitution and these he would dislike and he would giggle about plants he considered vulgar. Cedric was often amused by his plants and gave them human characteristics. Once he got me to smell a species of creeping sage from Portugal, asking me to identify its scent.

'What do you think of that?'

'Aniseed.'

'What else?' he asked. 'A whore sucking a bullseye!'

Cedric Morris was an exceptional plantsman, famous in the iris world. At one time he was growing a thousand tall bearded iris seedlings from his carefully recorded crosses each year. When the Americans went in for mass breeding of irises Cedric felt discouraged but went on making selected crosses. On his travels he found several previously unknown plants, such as a white phlomis from which he took cuttings, which unfortunately did not root. He claimed to have seen first *Cistus palhinhae* at Cape St Vincent in south-west Portugal and showed it to 'Cherry' Ingram. But Ingram always maintained the discovery was his own. Then there was *Narcissus minor* 'Cedric Morris', which was found by Basil Laing in Portugal where a road was being made and which was about to be lost. Laing met Cedric and gave him some bulbs. This plant is remarkable in that it had never been found before and has never been seen since growing in the wild. It flowers at Christmas and Beth Chatto presented Cedric with a lovely pan of it during his ninetieth birthday celebration lunch at Jenny Robinson's.

When you arrived at Benton End you never knew who would be

Cedric Morris: *St Helena*, 1965. Oil on canvas. 76 x 51 cm. Minories.

On his travels he found several previously unknown plants …

There was an atmosphere of rustic sophistication.

there, Natalie Bevan, Randolph Churchill or Vita Sackville-West among many others. Cedric and Vita were well acquainted. She grew a lot of his bearded irises at Sissinghurst (though she later gave them up as they tended to need staking too much) and Cedric had some of her old roses. Cedric described her as 'a great lady who never lost her integrity', this with reference to her son's book about her marriage, which greatly upset him. Vita bought his painting, *The Entry of Moral Turpitude into New York Harbour* (1926). I met Kathleen Hale at Benton End too. Moggie Hale was an enormously amusing lady, a great friend of the painter Joan Warburton, known always as Maudie. Joan's nickname had been bestowed on her by Lett who, seeing her peering out through a window one day, called out, 'Come into the garden, Maud.' Moggie sent a telegram to Maudie when her son was born saying, 'Congratulations, Maudie. Has it a twig or hasn't it?' Maudie's baby was promptly nicknamed Twig.

The excitement of Benton End swallowed me up, its ambience, the talk, scandal too, the people, Millie and the cats and Cedric's tales. During my winter visits Cedric would sit by the fireside and in a voice sometimes almost inaudible, as if thinking aloud, recollect the past – his mother, an aunt who rode side-saddle from Wales to London, and so much more. When I first went there, even in 1971, it seemed very different from anywhere else I had known and extraordinarily continental and civilised. There was an atmosphere of rustic sophistication. It wasn't just the building; it was Cedric's personality. When he died the house died with him. He was absolutely entertaining, though he did not suffer fools gladly. If he disliked people sometimes he would not speak at all. One day when I arrived I found Cedric with a garden visitor. He muttered to me, 'I must get rid of this ghastly woman,' and he directed me to put a clump of *Dracunculus vulgaris*, which the lady had admired, into her motor. It was a hot day and the plant would certainly have stunk the car out. Cedric would, on the other hand, value greatly other good gardeners.

He urged me to see 'the best astrantias' in John Aldridge's garden at Great Bardfield and I drove him several times to see his friends, including John Nash at Bottengoms Farm.

I would often stay for memorable meals, gourmet feasts with wine and olives and so on which Millie cooked. (By that time Lett, who was not in good health, kept himself aloof from Cedric's gardening friends.) Although Cedric tended to get upset if I talked about his pictures, I had always had an interest in British painters, especially of the 1920–70 period. Cedric's paintings reflected a great deal of his personality. What he strove for in his irises was there in the pictures in his extraordinary colour sense. The colours were so singular they made your eyes pop. There was a solid integrity to his painting which I admired and have gone on admiring. When sorting through a cupboard one day, looking for seeds, with Cedric directing the search, a rolled, rotting canvas fell out. 'That should have been thrown away years ago. Lucky we have a bonfire.' I protested. It was a landscape, *Drought, Oxfordshire, 1933* and Cedric said, 'Put it in your car; it's a failed picture.'

'A garden is either right or not right; I don't know why.'

With his sympathy and discernment for plants Cedric helped to train my eye and sharpen my critical faculty. He would say, 'A garden is either right or not right; I don't know why.' Benton End was a garden that was right.

John Morley

John Morley studied at Beckenham Art School, Ravensbourne College of Art and the Royal Academy Schools and he has taught at Epsom School of Art, Suffolk College and the Royal Academy Schools. His paintings and engravings are exhibited regularly in galleries and at art fairs in London and abroad and his work is included in displays at The Museum of Modern Art, Wales, Machynlleth, Powys and in several public collections. He was elected a Brother of the Art Workers' Guild in 1990 and he was invited to become a member of the Society of Wood Engravers in 1996. John Morley has a large garden in north Suffolk where he specialises in the cultivation of snowdrops.

A neighbour of mine, Elizabeth Smart the writer, first introduced me to Benton End during the mid-1970s. My first impression of the house was of its wonderful colours with its blue doors and walls of earthy Venetian red massed with euphorbias. I got on very well with Cedric and after that first time I regularly visited him on Thursday evenings after my teaching. Whenever I rang to see if it was convenient for me to come, Lett,whom I scarcely got to know, would answer and say, 'Oh yes, Cedric always likes to see you.' I can remember only one occasion when Lett very reluctantly walked in the garden, under

Cedric Morris: *Portimao, Algarve*. Oil on canvas. 51 x 61 cm. Minories.

strict doctor's orders to get some fresh air. Cedric and I would walk round the garden talking about plants. Before supper we would drink wonderful whisky (I remember that John Skeaping had sent Cedric a case) and then I would stay overnight, have a beautiful meal cooked by Millie and be entertained by all Cedric's stories. I met so many people at Benton End – Archie Gordon, Tony Venison, Ronnie Blythe, Beth Chatto and numerous others, many of whom became lifelong friends. I regret never having met John Nash, who also came on Thursdays, but who had always left before my arrival.

Cedric's garden gave me an amazing buzz. I hadn't seen a garden quite like it before. It was like an Alpine meadow, a magical place for a plantsman, full of source material, exciting for the knowledge you could gain from it. Cedric was not particularly interested in arranging plants, only in placing them where they grew happily, yet the

Cedric's garden ... was like an Alpine meadow, a magical place for a plantsman ...

He made you feel that you were the most important person in the world.

effect was always aesthetically pleasing. It felt wonderfully free, a bit of Provence in an English garden. Cedric was immensely generous, both with his knowledge and with gifts of plants, whole clumps of them, though he would shudder when 'blue-haired lady gardeners with notebooks' bore down on him. I have many of his plants, especially fritillaries, in my garden now and have passed hundreds to other gardeners. In the years that I knew Cedric his sight was beginning to fail. Sometimes when I arrived I would find him in the garden pulling up orchids instead of weeds, thinking they were grass, but I would tease him about it. He enjoyed being teased.

It was years before I talked with Cedric about art, though his paintings have had a great influence upon me. I particularly admired the incredible strength and sense of design of his flower paintings and studies of still life with landscape background. I was able to take him to shows in Bury St Edmunds and Colchester and to his ninetieth birthday show in London. He hated London (though in years gone by he had once ridden a horse there for Johnnie Skeaping to use as a model) but he came to see a picture of mine in the Royal Academy Summer Show. He wore a black velvet dinner jacket and carried a gold-topped cane and the porters made way for him as he came up the stairs. As always, he said little, just looked at my painting and came away, but I was pleased and honoured by his visit. Cedric desperately wanted to see Wales again and I hoped to be able to take him to the Gower. Sadly he died before I could do so.

After Cedric's death I came across a thank-you letter from Edward Bawden to Cedric. This led me in 1992 to paint a picture as a tribute to Edward Bawden to which I gave the quotation, 'A Generous Quantity of Box'. Bawden had obviously received a characteristically generous present. Cedric was generous with his time too, always making himself available and never too busy to give you his full attention. He made you feel that you were the most important person in the world.

Daphne Clark

The late Daphne Clark good-humouredly cleaned the house for Cedric and Lett for many years and became their loyal friend.

A Mrs Morris asked me to phone Lett because he needed help as Cecil, the manservant, had gone back to St Helena. Lett said, 'We'll talk about money later. All I want is Sir Cedric's bed made as he is due home from abroad.' So I did. I recall them both standing at the door at 2.00 pm to welcome me. They both bowed courteously. They said they recognised me, probably from a Red Cross Open Day there.

Of course I had to do more than make up the bed. I cleaned for them two afternoons a week. The place was filthy and full of flies and lacewings upstairs. I had to put a cloth on to soak the thick coating of grime off the newel posts. In Lett's room I cleaned the windows at the back view. There was no putty so the glass fell out. 'Woe, woe!' said Lett. But they were lovely sunny days. I remember the things on Lett's desk, a crystal shaped like a peach stone (I believe they take years to form) and a lovely china lion on the window-sill. I cleaned the bath and made the guest room ready. There was a big bed called the Marriage Bed. I used to wash Sir Cedric's corduroy trousers. Lucy's paintings were all mouldy. I scrubbed them!

Lett Haines: *Two Figures*, Cartoon for oil painting, 1923. Mixed media. 45 x 45 cm. Private collection.

There was plenty of dry rot at Benton End and sometimes there were mice in the pantry but I took the condition of the house in my stride. I'd been in service in some very funny houses and I'd been a Land Girl and I was used to basic conditions. I'd always read a lot, like Patrick Leigh Fermor's travel books where you read about basic standards. Anyway my sister's an artist and I liked the atmosphere. Mind you, if you stayed at Benton End you had to become resistant to microbes. I couldn't eat there – I'd be ill. I'd bring my own mug. Natalie Bevan used to bring her own lunch in a dish when she came. There were lots of flies and there was a huge stone sink with rather nice tiles they'd brought from abroad, but the draining board was vile and as for the plate rack . . . ! All the bitumen was worn white on the shower and there was no shower curtain.

There was never much money. When I asked Lett for some money to buy Vim he said, 'Daphne, I believe you eat the stuff,' and when Millie (Hayes) had to ask me to accept less money, Lett hid away from me. Once Lett left me a note saying, 'Herewith cheque for 60/–. The ceiling has fallen down in classroom. Mr Tricker may be along.'

Sir Cedric was a real gentleman. We shared the same sense of humour. Sir Cedric liked to visit Mum and give her daffodil bulbs called Angel's Tears. He used to ask if she would wear her pink hat and coat when she came to Benton End. I went to Cardiff on the train to his Retrospective Exhibition. He was on the same train but I didn't know that at the time. In my diary of 1977 I noted that I made berberis jelly for him and that I read John Skeaping's book to him.

Lett too was charming in his own way. At least he was always charming to me. He did a cookery programme for Anglia TV. The cameras took up a lot of room in the kitchen and he couldn't get round the table to get a wooden spoon. He was very upset that he had to stir with a metal one because of what people would think. He wouldn't get out of bed if it was garden people visiting but once when I was up in Lett's room a Rolls came up the drive and it was a man in a dirty old raincoat, Lucian Freud.

Cedric Morris: Still Life before Sussex fireback (Detail), see p. 108.

Very elegant people with trilby hats and very expensive tweed suits glared at me.

When they had guests for lunch there was generally an argument, Cedric at the top end of the table and Lett at the kitchen end. One Christmas they all came out one at a time with their plates before the pudding, playing a game kissing the maid – me. I once had to take a tray out to people who were visiting because Millie was too scared to go out. There were fancy biscuits, fancy plates and the best cups and saucers. Very elegant people with trilby hats and very expensive tweed suits glared at me. It was Hinge and Bracket. Once I was cleaning out the drain under the manhole with rods when an Alvis came down the drive. It was Sidney Nolan. There was a glorious pong. Sir Cedric said, 'It will do him a power of good'.

Cedric Morris: *Quinces and Nerines* (Detail), see p. 60.

Michael Lloyd

Michael Lloyd was Cedric's cousin. His father was a soldier in the days when the army rode horses and as a small boy he trotted on his pony behind the troop horses wondering why he couldn't keep up. This interest developed so slowly that at an age when his contemporaries had long retired he rode for two seasons over fences and hurdles, providing hilarious entertainment for those onlookers who had not backed the horse he was riding. He rode Game Purston in the 1970 Grand National but the next year the horse's lameness meant that he gave up his attempts as a jockey, rather to the relief of those who found themselves riding alongside. He then concentrated on sculpting racehorses, but the factor of providing hilarious entertainment to the onlookers remained a constant. Cedric provided great encouragement but in later years his failing sight shielded him from the worst excesses. Michael Lloyd's work has been exhibited in London, Paris, New York, Geneva and anywhere else he can persuade a gallery to accept it.

Lett Haines: *Vereda Tropicale*. Watercolour, pigment and adhesives on paper. 77 x 57 cm. Private collection.

The earliest I heard of Cedric was his show at the Leicester Gallery. He had exhibited a number of nudes where few details were left to the imagination and my grandmother spent the entire Private View turning them face to the wall. But it was on my first arrival at Benton End that Cedric's legendary ability to make every guest feel at home was put to its severest test. He talked about art, but found that it went straight over my head. He talked about gardening and drew a blank at that. As I looked into his eyes I could see him searching desperately for some subject that would draw a spark of interest from the inert figure that he saw slumped before him. At last he found a topic that brought a reaction from his listener – the 'goings-on' of the Morris relations who, even in the relaxed atmosphere of the reign of Edward VII, nevertheless sent a frisson through the respectability in South Wales.

I could see him searching desperately for some subject that would draw a spark of interest.

There was Henry, who, for a time, was Chairman of a bank in Swansea. Even under the undemanding accountancy regulations of the Companies Act 1854, he so rearranged the figures on the Profit and Loss that he was sent down for a stretch of two years.

Robert's interest was in figures of a different sort. He resembled a seventeenth-century admiral who lived in a huge house with a large number of male servants. And whenever he was angry with them, which was often, he would shout at them and call them bastard or cuckold, for which he could personally vouch. Robert so liberally exercised what in the Middle Ages would have been called *droit du seigneur* that throughout the villages of South Wales and the West of England I can claim more blood relations than most people could find in a generation. Those were his extra-mural activities. For the main curriculum he had a wife who lay desperately ill on the first floor. But while the wife lay ill on the first floor, he kept on the ground floor what in the jargon of the day was termed a fancy woman. Eventually the wife died and the fancy woman went to the funeral dressed in the wife's jewellery; all the wife's jewellery. Not just a pair of earrings and a brooch, but every pair of earrings and every brooch were pinned to some corner of the lady's anatomy. Thus attired, she marched in pole position behind the funeral.

Cedric Morris: *Landscape at Newlyn*, 1919.
Oil on canvas. 30 x 34 cm. Private collection.

Armin had no interest in figures of any sort. As a young man in

Cedric Morris: *Llangynofor Bridge*, 1934. Oil on canvas. 54 x 67 cm. Minories.

Armin … used to run race meetings on the downs outside Newbury.

the early nineteen hundreds he was given £10,000 to get him through his first year of adulthood. Although this might have been a quarter of a million by today's values, he spent it all in the first month. He later invested the proceeds of the Industrial Revolution in South Wales in a manner to ensure that the whisky distillery business would remain a profitable industry for many years to come. With those few drops that remained undrunk he used to run race meetings on the downs outside Newbury. These were wildly popular. They were popular with owners and trainers because if they had a horse that was a difficult ride, or had no chance, or was frankly dangerous, there was never any difficulty in finding a jockey to ride it. And they were popular with jockeys for a reason that I myself have never been able to find on any other British racecourse. It was that the jockeys engaged to ride on the following day were accommodated in the same wing as the female members of the racecourse staff.

Much of the best of The Pound and Benton End was over by the time I knew Cedric, but as a visitor for only a couple of nights a year I was impressed by the legion of old friends who would come to visit him. I would have found so many visitors exhausting, but Cedric thrived on them and we all drew reward from his company.

Many of the visitors I forgot; some I had heard of before. Following my experience with Cedric I was able to say to Beth Chatto that I knew nothing about gardening, then to Francis Bacon and later to Lucian Freud that I knew nothing about painting. There was an opera singer to whom I admitted no knowledge of music, so it was with a practised phrase when I sat next to Elizabeth David that I said I knew nothing about food. It is better to say you can't swim than to founder out of your depth. But this early training stood me in good stead, and when I sat next to a Colonel in MI6 I could say that I knew nothing about the Secret Service. He seemed to feel that this was as it should be.

He had been ordered to sit at a table in some desert-bound drinking haunt with a crumpled-up piece of paper on the table. He sat there throughout the day as travellers came and went and a filthy beggar covered in sores squatted lifelessly in the corner. Towards the end of the evening the beggar shuffled past the table and the paper was gone. Many years later a pin-striped Englishman came up to him in his club in London. 'You don't remember me,' he said. 'I was the beggar at that café and I still haven't got rid of the sores. But you made life difficult for me. If you hadn't sat at a centre table I could have got away quicker.'

Cedric too was once approached by the Foreign Office. A man in black coat and striped trousers arrived at Benton End and asked him to go to some Mediterranean country, mingle with the people and ask their opinions.

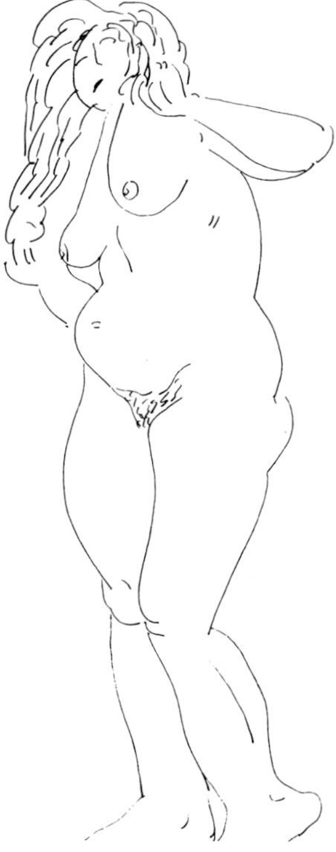

Cedric Morris: *Standing Nude*, 1924.

It is better to say you can't swim than to founder out of your depth.

'I couldn't possibly afford the fare,' said Cedric.

'We'll put you ashore from a destroyer,' came the answer.

'I'm just a painter and gardener,' said Cedric, 'nothing to do with politics.'

'Just the person who would be least suspected,' was the reply.

'How did you hear of me?' asked Cedric.

'One year when you were painting abroad you went to the consul to get money. After that we kept tabs on you. We always keep a watch on people who go abroad for long periods. You should do this for your country.'

'I'm a very unpatriotic man,' said Cedric.

Benton End was best visited in summer . . .

Benton End was best visited in summer. A stalwart attempt to block up draughts in the windows did not last long, but installing a door behind Cedric's head checked the wind slightly as it came straight in from the garden. Insulation in the roof brought the temperature up a few degrees.

Lett had unwisely installed a 'sit-up-and-beg' bath rather than the normal lie-back-and-wallow variety. One poor lady was too broad amidships and got stuck. Lett had to climb in the bathroom window by a ladder, and to her excruciating embarrassment, a platoon of male helpers got her out. Even for those unstuck it was miserably uncomfortable and only your ankles were covered in hot water. Its height was a navigational hazard and even the addition of a step did no more than make it bearable.

The spare bedroom had an internal window onto the passage with a thin curtain across it, and at the foot of the bed was a wardrobe with a mirror in the door – left over from loftier days I think. Clean sheets for the bed came from the linen cupboard, sometimes the only warm place in the house. This had not gone unnoticed by other residents and in the earlier days it was full of bats hanging from the walls, every one of them asleep and comfortably warm. But then they went. Perhaps one winter it was too cold for them too.

Maggi Hambling

Maggi Hambling was first Artist in Residence at the National Gallery in 1980, and joint winner with Patrick Caulfield of the Jerwood Prize for Painting in 1995. Her public collections in Britain include The British Museum, Tate, National Portrait Gallery and Scottish National Gallery of Modern Art. Her memorial to Oscar Wilde was unveiled in 1998 behind the church of St Martin in the Fields.

I first realised that I could possibly become an artist when I was fourteen and at Amberfield School in Nacton, near Ipswich. I managed to do a painting in the last ten minutes of an art exam during which I had otherwise done nothing but flick paint at other girls and eye the teacher with whom I was madly in love. Without even trying I had come top in art, whereas my experience of maths was the opposite. I had failed to pass the entrance exam to Ipswich High School.

I was given a lot of encouragement by Yvonne Drewry, the art teacher, but my parents needed some reassurance that becoming an artist was a good idea, so in 1960 I took my first two oil paintings to what was known in Hadleigh as the 'Artists' House'. Lett answered the door and replied to my request to see Sir Cedric that he was having his dinner. I asked if I could wait and was amazed to see Lett

Lett Haines: *Regardant*, 1959. Mixed media. Height 17.5 cm. Private collection.

bringing dish after dish to the long kitchen table. Cedric was friendly and charming. I propped up my paintings and received encouraging, though completely contradictory, criticisms from each of them. I finally left what in Hadleigh was considered a notorious house at nine-thirty in the evening. My mother thought I had been sold into the white slave trade.

I was still at school but Lett asked me if I would like to come and paint during the holidays so I arrived on the first morning after the end of term. I was too shy to knock so I sat in the ditch outside the gates and painted there. Lucy Harwood called me in for elevenses and that was the beginning. Alan Brooks, known as 'China', was the regular helper in the kitchen but when he was not there I helped Lett. He was a harsh critic, especially of my ways in the kitchen, and I was often reduced to tears by the end of the week, but his excuse was, 'You don't pick holes in a rotten apple.' I sometimes had to scrape maggots off the meat as there were lots of flies in the kitchen and the fridge, placed next to the Aga, was less than efficient. Still, I was accepted; I found a card on the seat of my donkey which said, 'This seat is still hot from the seat of Maggi Soop,' and I have been known as Maggi rather than Margaret ever since.

Lett was my mentor and he it was who taught me the importance of the imagination. He told me that I should get my work into the relationship of being my best friend and that art had to be the absolute priority of one's life. These are the most important things anyone has ever said to me and I have lived by them.

Lett … taught me the importance of the imagination …

Cedric encouraged me to draw, but I felt that Cedric's students often had a tendency to paint as he did, whereas Lett had the ability to address himself to a new person and bring out what *you* were. He encouraged one's spirit of independence as an artist. The art world can be pretty frightful so it is essential to do what you have to do and bugger other people! Lett had an enormous personality and capacity as a teacher so I learned a lot about art in our conversations in the

He encouraged experiment too . . .

Lett Haines: *Witch Fetish: Portrait of Maggi Soop*, 1962. Mixed media. Height 14 cm. Private collection.

kitchen. Nothing was trotted out as a formula and if he couldn't answer a question he was quite prepared to say that he didn't know. He was constantly experimenting in his own work, always responding to everything that was going on and never throwing a thing away in case he could use it in a sculpture. He encouraged experiment too, advising me to try my idea in another medium whenever I got stuck.

Cedric was more hermetic as a teacher. He had certain ideas which he would pass on, as when he criticised my painting of a neck, 'Remember, it is always a column,' but Lett wouldn't do this. Cedric would sometimes take me into his bedroom and ask me to go through his paintings to decide what to destroy. We would take half a dozen out but he never got rid of any of them and back they would go. Lett had put Cedric in the position of Master Artist and himself as his impresario, cossetting him in such a way that he could live in his own world and not have to look after himself at all.

Lett Haines: *Fat Laugh*. Height 10cm Private collection.

Cedric resented it if Lett sat down to eat with everyone because he was often drunk and, when drunk, could be very entertaining, taking all the attention away from Cedric. Lett, however, was socially vulnerable. He devoted lots of time to bed and the bottle. He would grumble, when preparing one of his extravagant meals, 'The buggers don't know what they're eating. They might as well have ham sandwiches.' His conversation was highly sophisticated, well laced with sex which he brought into almost everything. He 'communed with God' in the afternoons and I would draw him as he lay in bed. He loved to go out in his 'best frock' (a dark blue suit) and was a very good dancer. There were some wonderful moments, like the time when Elizabeth David visited and Lett took her on a grand tour of the larder and butler's pantry. He took off the silver lid from a tray of 'cold collations' and out flew a moth. Then there was the time when Lucy (Harwood) introduced Lett to someone at The Minories as, 'This is Cedric Morris's um … er …,' which he strongly objected to.

I had seven years of art training in the glorious sixties when there were grants for students. I went to Ipswich School of Art, Camberwell and the Slade, all of which gave me the time to work, but nothing was ever like Benton End. Lett was a second father to me and Benton End made me who I am. My mother once said, 'I wish to goodness you'd never set foot in Benton End,' but it was too late.

… nothing was ever like Benton End.

Joanna Carrington

Joanna Carrington is the daughter of Noel Carrington who began and edited Puffin Picture Books for children. She was educated at Monkton Wild School, the Fernand Léger Atelier in Paris and the Central School of Art and has taught at Hornsey and Chelsea Schools of Art. Joanna Carrington regularly exhibits her paintings at art fairs and galleries in England and France. Her latest exhibition was in 1999 at the Thackeray Gallery, London. She has published Landscape Painting for Beginners *(Studio Vista, 1970) and a children's book,* Pepper and Jam *(Jonathan Cape). Joanna Carrington and her husband, Christopher Mason, live in France.*

I arrived at Benton End alone by train and bus at the age of sixteen, with very few clothes or art materials and feeling rather nervous. Immediately I was hurled into a completely new world of grown-ups with no rules and no apparent concerns.

On my first morning Cedric taught me how to stretch, size and prime a canvas and, I think, how to lay out colours and one or two other technical details, but after that I was left alone, free to paint in the studio or garden or out in the fields and to develop in my own way. In fact, I can't recall any teaching at all, but occasionally Cedric would tilt his head to one side, remove his pipe and say, 'Good,

good'. I think he did give a little more time to the old ladies who came every summer in search of encouragement and he certainly gave a lot of his attention to any young male students who were, I seem to remember, mostly Welsh.

Cedric did, however, show me by example the value of hard work. I went into his studio one morning and there he was, working on a large still life with irises that was propped against the wall. He was working on the lower bit so was sitting, uncomfortably, it seemed to me, on an upturned flower pot, with his palette on the floor. He had not heard me come in, so I watched him for a long while, amazed at his confidence and concentration. Then Lett bustled in to upbraid him for not delivering the lettuces and leeks from the garden for lunch and Cedric laid down his brushes at once.

Lunch was excellent and often a very noisy and hilarious affair. Being particularly naïve, it never struck me that Cedric and Lett were lovers and I had no idea what camp humour was all about. Lett would waltz in and out of the dining room bearing various exotic dishes and hurl what sounded like abuse at Cedric, who would giggle or return fire. Lett's tongue was as sharp as a needle and I was rather scared of him. Whether or not his pink complexion was due to drink I was too inexperienced to tell; perhaps cooking over a hot stove was the cause. He never ate with us or even in the kitchen. He made sandwiches and took them in a pale cream tin to his bedroom, where he would stay all afternoon with the door wide open.

... I did learn from him to be bold with colour and imaginative in my choice of subject matter.

Cedric was always kind and gentle with me. He put my work into the Colchester summer art show, and even bought one of my paintings – *Onions Hanging on a Tree*. This was greatly encouraging. I think I did learn from him to be bold with colour and imaginative in my choice of subject matter. However, I disliked his – and some of the students' – use of thick paint, especially when applied with a palette knife. I determined never to work in that way.

That long and happy summer gave me the chance to indulge in

Cedric Morris: *Dragonmouth*, 1933. Oil on canvas. 67 x 55 cm. Private collection.

the one thing I loved doing the most. It was a precious interlude before being launched into Paris and the loneliness and rigours of the Fernand Léger Atelier. I never went back to Benton End and I'm sorry I didn't. Living abroad made it difficult but whenever I had an exhibition in London I'd receive a good-luck letter or a telegram from Cedric and Lett.

Anne Coghill

The late Anne Coghill read History at Newnham College, Cambridge and studied art at St John's Wood School run by Pat Millard, who later became head of Camberwell School of Art. John Minton was also a pupil, a shy young man who would turn up each Monday with an armful of enormous paintings which he had worked on over the weekend. After a period of teaching in Wales, Anne went into youth work, specialising in dramatic work with children, including an annual Youth Drama Festival. She spent the next twelve years organising art and drama at Claybury Mental Hospital in Essex and later qualified as a psychologist. More recently she was active in animal welfare and was instrumental in encouraging supermarkets to stock free-range eggs. Anne Coghill painted and wrote articles and poems.

My friend Con Morgan and I were regular weekend visitors to Benton End from 1948 until the 1970s. Con was always the centre of talk, laughter and gaiety, whereas I was so inhibited that I didn't know how to respond to all the interesting people that were constantly coming and going there. Once Cedric placed a rose on my breast saying, 'This is where the rose wants to be,' but I was so paralysed with shyness, I could say nothing in reply.

Lett Haines: *Jardin d'artiste*, 1969. Mixed media. 60 x 35 cm. Private collection.

This pattern was repeated when Cedric came to stay with me in London for a couple of nights. He took me out to dine at the Establishment Club. I had looked forward to it, but when there, we sat sadly wondering how to get the conversation going; to my relief there was a cabaret to distract us. We were two bundles of energy dammed up in childhood and rendered voiceless!

Nevertheless I did respond to the magic of Benton End and particularly to the beautiful garden where I did my painting and where Cedric's love of plants shone out. Whereas Con belonged socially at Benton End, I belonged as a painter.

Cedric helped me with the arrangement of colour and with composition, but as I began to develop in my own way, becoming interested in rather abstract and unconventional approaches in my painting, it was Lett who gave me advice. What helped me most, however, was the atmosphere at Benton End which encouraged me to be free to be myself. For someone as painfully shy as I was, this was not easy.

Benton End was full of humour, liveliness, drama, creativity and a sense of freedom and the food, cooked by Lett, was lovely. I accepted it as a fascinating place. Most wonderful to me was to find a couple who perfectly complemented each other in the running of the School, a gay couple whose enduring love, wit and humour had enabled them to win through to stability. They were like rocks to each other.

I can remember Cedric looking out of the car window and calling out, 'I can see three pictures!' as I was driving him home from Beth Chatto's after what was probably his last visit there. In spite of his difficulties he never complained but remained interested in life to the end.

Benton End could not have survived without Cedric's and Lett's charisma. The hellebores, a gift from Cedric, which are doing so well in my garden, are a reminder of Benton End and a time when my life was enriched enormously.

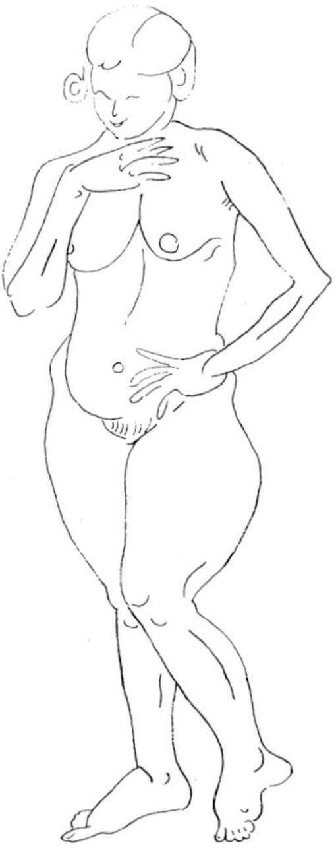

Cedric Morris: *Standing Nude*, 1924.

Benton End was full of humour, liveliness, drama, creativity and a sense of freedom ...

Ashe Ericksson

Ashe Ericksson studied at Ipswich School of Art, specialising in gilding illuminated miniatures. She now works as a muralist and interior designer. She lives in Suffolk.

Sometime in the 1960s I was introduced to Benton End and would go there to do some botanical drawings for which I had been commissioned. Cedric gave me permission to draw by the pond provided I didn't disturb the breeding frogs. I remember I shared a liking with Cedric for weeds such as the giant hogweeds by the pond.

Benton End seemed like fairyland to me, as if real life did not exist. Cedric and Lett gave me the licence to be myself so that I no longer felt an oddity as I had always done. They too were so obviously different and Cedric's free and encouraging approach and his habit of laughing at life were a pivotal influence on me.

Afternoons at Benton End followed a strict ritual. Even though we had actually seen Cedric first painting near the gate, we had to pretend to be visiting Lett first as he was jealous of any attention given to Cedric. He would be lying in his chaotic bedroom with champagne and biscuits and with empty bottles lined up round the side of the bed. All his cloaks – and he had beautiful clothes – were bunched together almost horizontally on the same hook. His table was the ironing board, never, as far as I could see, used for ironing, but piled high with cigar boxes covered in little sculptures. These were constructed from crab shells or from vegetables first baked hard in the oven and given glass eyes from the dolls' hospital. These were very surreal and they undoubtedly had an influence on my own idiosyncratic type of work.

Cedric, by contrast with Lett, was very tidy. His room was like a monk's cell, simple and plain with a white coverlet on the bed and his drawings stashed neatly under it. But he too had a sense of bawdy fun. I remember in his studio he had a huge stuffed elephant's penis stretched to its limit and blackened with age like a Roman pillar. Elegant ladies leaned against it and said, 'Oh Cedric, do tell us what this is.' 'A glans penis from a bull elephant,' he would reply and be delighted by their response.

Cedric and Lett were a creative force in my life …

The food at Benton End, served on wooden platters, was elegant but terrifying. I used to wonder if I would live through the night or at least hallucinate after an evening meal of grey fungus stew which emerged from the mouldy kitchen with its copper sink and drainer and its baskets of fruit from the garden, gradually deliquescing from still life to Damien Hirst. Yet cheese and butter would arrive from Fortnums by train!

Cedric and Lett were a creative force in my life, even though I was never an actual student of the school. Artists need the stimulus of other artists like that; theirs are the voices that have gone before to inform one's own judgement.

John Norris Wood

John Norris Wood trained at Goldsmiths College, the East Anglian School of Painting and Drawing and the Royal College of Art. He is a freelance artist, printmaker and illustrator and Visiting Professor responsible for Natural History Illustration and Ecological Studies at the Royal College of Art. He wrote the successful Nature Hide and Seek *Books for children, and has written and broadcast on natural history subjects for television, including the* Life on Earth *series. John Norris Wood has exhibited his work at galleries and museums in London and abroad and has been on numerous expeditions and field trips all over the world. He was one of the British artists chosen for the Living Earth Expedition to Venezuela. When not on trips to the Galapagos, Ecuador or Rwanda, John Norris Wood lives and works on his own small nature reserve in Sussex. His interests are equally divided between art and conservation and he is actively involved both with students and on his own in several conservation organisations.*

I was introduced to Benton End in about 1952 by Edward Bawden. It was a place that was full of fun (and not a little cantankerousness) which placed art at the centre of things and assumed that artists were really important and necessary to society. The house itself was beautiful with its mysterious dark and rambling passages, uneven floors, its studios and 'cheek-to-cheek' bedrooms. The garden was full of the best flowers imaginable, especially the bearded irises, and was an Eden to me, warm, protected and complete with European green tree frogs which Cedric had imported and which especially delighted me.

Part of the pleasure of Benton End was the endless stream of artists and other visitors of all ages. I remember particularly Glyn Morgan, Rosemary Russell, Lord Longford, Maudie O'Malley (Joan Warburton), Lucy Harwood, Eileen Mayo, John Nash and 'Arsehole Brooks', Lett's name for the eminent bowel cancer surgeon.

I found Cedric's love of and sympathy for animals very endearing.

I was very fond of both Lett and Cedric, though I found it easier to get to know the more communicative Lett. His work was eccentric and witty and he was a bloody good draughtsman. Both he and Cedric were creatively amusing in their different ways and I must admit to having been much entertained by their often silly tiffs. Both were good, straightforward, though unorthodox tutors when one could persuade them into that frame of mind. At first I found the naïve qualities of Cedric's paintings rather strange, but gradually, steadily, I came to appreciate them, then love and admire them greatly. I think Cedric made an important contribution to British painting both as a wonderful colourist who was brilliant at getting the 'vibes' of his subject, be it flowers, landscapes or spicy portraits and as a teacher of artists such as Lucian Freud, Christopher Wood, Lucy Harwood and many others. I consider his work to be sadly neglected and undervalued.

I found Cedric's love of and sympathy for animals very endearing. We had many conversations about the terrible destruction of wildlife in East Anglia and especially of birds with toxic sprays. Out of this concern came one of the first environmental protest paintings, *Landscape of Shame* c.1960, though an even earlier painting, *Shags* 1938 depicts birds looking disgustedly at a tanker on the skyline leaking oil.

Cedric Morris: *Wood Pigeons* (Detail), see p. 72.

Benton End had an enormous, mainly joyful and liberating influence on me, opening up all sorts of avenues and experiences, though I never felt tempted towards homosexuality. I remember it with tremendous affection. It was the best art school in its maverick way that I have ever come across and I loved it all.

Elizabeth Wright

After school in Oxford and lessons at Oxford Art School Elizabeth 'Bod' Wright took a domestic science course at Atholl Crescent. She has been at various times cook at Eton College, model, usherette and Land Army girl, always endeavouring to keep up her painting at the same time. She has recently taken a number of further education courses including a degree in English at the University of East Anglia. She enjoys travelling in Europe and lives for half the year in France where she pursues her interest in wild flowers. She also enjoys passive anthropology, by which she means sitting in cafés and taverns watching the world go by. Elizabeth Wright is a member of the Norwich 20 Group.

My father was a doctor in Bristol. My nursery, presided over by a nanny, was directly above the surgery so I always had to be very quiet, beautifully turned out in my Liberty dresses and healthy, as an ill child would not have been a good advertisement for a doctor. It never occurred to me to disobey my parents.

In my teens I had to look after my mother during an illness and when she was convalescing we went to live with my grandmother. In return for my care, my mother, who had met Cedric at a party in

Cedric Morris: *Pound Farm*, 1933.
Oil on canvas. 60 x 73 cm. Minories.

London, paid for me to go to Benton End for about seven months during the years 1946–7. I went to be vetted by Lett beforehand and had to stay overnight with Lucy Harwood because the road was flooded.

The contrast between Benton End and my grandparents' home was unbelievable. They were Plymouth Brethren and there was a restrictive and claustrophobic atmosphere in the house despite its modern, light decor. The days were always highly ordered. There was a place for everything and everything in its place and there was not a speck of dust anywhere. I was expected to go to Plymouth Brethren meetings wearing a hat and, horror of horrors, I hadn't got one! Life there was hardly conducive to painting. I tried once and got paint on the oakwood banisters. At Benton End, however, I had such a sense of freedom. In the downstairs lavatory Lett had the nicknames of previous students pasted on the wall using cut-out letters from magazines. My nickname was Body and it was a great day when I saw 'Body' on the wall. I felt then that I truly belonged, and was accepted for what I was. It was as if this was what I had been waiting for all my life.

It was as if this was what I had been waiting for all my life.

It is hard to describe the atmosphere. People of all ages from different backgrounds were students or day visitors and though sometimes, when no other students were staying, I was alone with Cedric and Lett constantly warring like an old married couple, I could cope with that. The food, cooked by Lett, was wonderful and we were surrounded by art. The feel of the place was a whole new experience.

I am a natural rebel and don't like being told what to do in relation to painting, but Cedric and Lett did not want to influence me, only to encourage me to get on with it without interference. I always hated being watched or my picture being looked at while it evolved. It was only when it was finished (though knowing when to stop and call a painting finished is also a problem) that I could bear it to be looked at and receive constructive criticism. This could be immensely helpful when it came from people like Lett and Cedric whose work I respected. Nevertheless, when I first started working in the commu-

Cedric Morris: *Tom Wright*, 1950. Oil on canvas. 59.5 x 39.5 cm. Minories.

Cedric was very methodical with his preparation for a painting ...

nal studio at Benton End it was a great ordeal, particularly as I had had virtually no art school training.

Cedric was very methodical with his preparation for a painting and this he considered very important. He mixed his colours on the palette beforehand, rarely using white so that he got clean, fresh colours. He taught me how to make and use zinc white and how to prepare the canvas properly. I painted non-stop and once Cedric suggested that I should give it a rest and do some drawing instead. He told me something I have always found valuable – that if you get stuck with a painting, you should prop it against a wall and look at it again in another three weeks, by which time it will be clear what to do with it. That has stopped me from destroying or over-painting pictures prematurely. Colour is all-important for me and Cedric was a superb colourist; I also tend to paint without pre-drawing, as Cedric did. He would come round to where I was painting once or twice a day and talk about what I was doing but he would never touch my work in any way. Cedric acted as if we students were like equals. Once he sent a message asking me if I could see him in the studio where he had been alone looking at my latest completed picture. I went, fearing that he was going to be angry with me over my escapades, but what he wanted to tell me was that I was finally becoming a painter. Those words could not have been better.

Cedric and Lett did their rounds of the studio separately. Lett talked more about drawing than painting. He taught me about how to use thick and thin lines to achieve solidity. He told me to look at my paintings in a mirror to help get the hang of perspective. Lett was, I think, more creative and avant-garde than Cedric, but there was a tragic drying up of his creativity later on. He tended to play a fatherly-motherly role with us younger students and he took a great, concerned interest in my love affairs. Once Lett asked me at the dinner table in front of a lot of older women students, 'Has your father sent you your batch of contraceptives yet?' I went pink with embarrassment.

Lett loved to shock and to stop Cedric getting all the attention. During the evening meal, Cedric would hold court at the head of the table and Lett, who would never eat with us, would bring in the food and make passing remarks just as he returned to the kitchen, like, 'Do you know that camels copulate backwards?' interrupting Cedric and stopping the conversation dead; but Cedric's conversation, too, was often bawdy especially on the rare occasions when he had had a few drinks.

It had been mooted that I should stay on at Benton End as a cook for the seven months during which the school was open. After all, I had been trained at Atholl Crescent in Edinburgh and had taken a job as a cook at one of the Houses at Eton, leaving only to nurse my mother. Much as I longed to stay on at Benton End I knew it would not be possible for me as I would have found it so frustrating to see everyone painting while I was in the kitchen. Once, however, when Lett was ill near the end of my stay, I had to manage the cooking for a week. I made a huge effort to live up to Lett's very high standards which everyone was used to. It was while there was still food rationing and afterwards Lett said that I had used up all his carefully accrued rations for a year! Lett did all the cooking himself with only some help with cleaning, washing up and so on from Mrs Ablett who lived in Hadleigh and who had had thirteen children. Everyone came through the kitchen, either to go into the garden or to go into the dining room and the general gathering place was Cedric's sitting room so Lett had a little cubby hole – a pantry outside the kitchen – to which he retired for a private drink. No doubt he needed it! He would say, 'I regret the day I boiled an egg for Mr Morris,' but he really looked after him. Lett rarely appeared on the scene until late in the morning. He would take a siesta after lunch and one of the students, Lucy, would take him tea in his bedroom. In later years, if you went to visit Benton End, you talked to Cedric first in the kitchen and then went up to Lett who held court in his bedroom. If he heard

'I regret the day I boiled an egg for Mr Morris.'

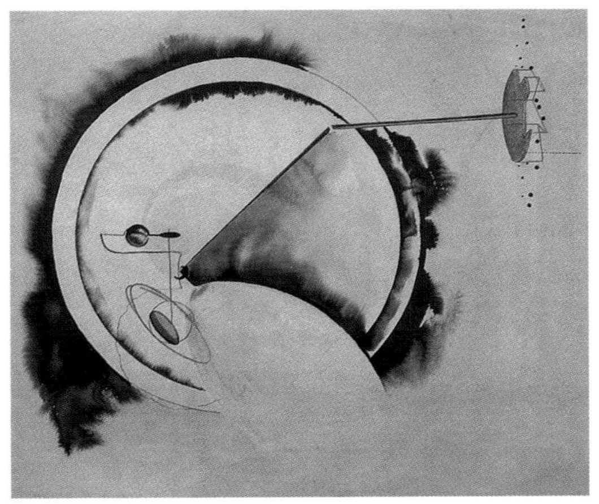

Lett Haines: *Conjectures*, 1921. Mixed media. 47 x 52 mm. Private collection.

you coming up the gravel drive, he would pop his head out of his bedroom window and greet you with his marvellous grin, but he would get jealous if you stayed too long with Cedric before seeing him.

Lett, I think, was a snob and much more conventional in his public role than Cedric and he was very concerned for the school's reputation, particularly its relationship to Hadleigh and the richer students and guests. My stepfather was known as Count van Horn (a title recently discovered to be bogus) so Lett always introduced my mother as the Countess van Horn and explained to me the importance of precedence when introducing women. It went like this: you always introduced the younger woman to the older unless the younger woman was titled and the older woman was not. It seemed to me to be somewhat hazardous if you were unsure of the ages or the status of either woman! Cedric seemed the freer spirit in our class-ridden society, though perhaps that was only possible because he was so wrapped in cotton wool by Lett.

Their manners were immensely courteous. Cedric, even when he was very frail, always came to the door to say goodbye and only went inside when we had reached the end of the drive. Even when he was not able to, he would attempt to get up from his chair when we left.

I met my future husband, Tom, at Benton End. He came from a poor family in Hadleigh and left school at fourteen. He met Lucian Freud in a pub in Hadleigh and it was Lucian who introduced Tom to Benton End. I remember Tom shinning down the drainpipe after we had been together in the attic, much to the puzzlement of Annie, a lady psychologist, who was keeping an eye out for any wrongdoing! Lett used to call Tom, who was five feet two inches, 'Tiny Mite' and he made up a poem which ended with the line 'He fell upon a buxom girl and disappeared from sight.'

The problem for a lot of students who stayed at Benton End was that sooner or later they had to leave this cushioned, not quite real world, go back to ordinary life and earn a living, as almost all the students were unable to earn their living by painting. I think that Cedric and Lett did not really understand how tough it was to be a painter and to keep up the standards they had set for us in the more conventional world outside the magic circle of Benton End which they had created. No doubt it had been a struggle for them, but their background was definitely advantageous to its creation. They knew the 'right' people when they needed them, possibly through their public-school education. Nevertheless, Cedric was a socialist and he taught poorer students for free. I think it was he who started the Labour Club in Hadleigh and he got Tom to restore and redecorate the rooms used by the Club.

Cedric Morris: *Woman with Earrings*, 1924.

Ronald Blythe

Ronald Blythe first visited Benton End shortly after World War II and he and Cedric Morris and Lett Haines became friends. He is a poet, essayist and literary critic, and his books include: The Age of Illusion, Akenfield, The View in Winter, William Hazlitt: Selected Writings, First Friends *and* Out of the Valley. *He has been given a number of literary awards, including the Society of Authors' Travel Scholarship and the Royal Society of Literature Heinemann Prize. His work has been translated and filmed. He lives in the house of his old friend John Nash at Wormingford, and has been associated with many East Anglian events connected with painting and literature.*

I was introduced to Benton End in 1948 by a writer friend, the poet and novelist, James Turner. He had bought the notorious haunted house, Borley Rectory, and was at the time teaching various friends in the neighbourhood how to grow mushrooms.

After that I visited Benton End frequently until Cedric's death in 1982. In 1956 after I had become a full-time writer and was doing some work for Benjamin Britten at Aldeburgh, I often stayed with John and Christine Nash at Bottengoms Farm in Wormingford. John would say, 'Let's go and see the boys,' and we would go to Benton End. Of course they would seem immensely old to me. I thought at the time I would like to be an artist but they knew I was really a writer and thought I would do a few writing chores for them.

Cedric and John Nash were old friends and fellow gardeners and would talk plants all the time. When Cedric came to Bottengoms John would say, 'What about artwork, old boy?' but then off they would go talking again about plants. Cedric always referred to himself as an artist-plantsman, which is what I put on his tombstone in Hadleigh cemetery. Cedric propagated irises in a shed in his garden. John disapproved of some of Cedric's iris species.

There were Iris Parties in June when hundreds of irises were in bloom inside the box hedges. Famous gardeners like Vita Sackville-West and other great plantsmen would turn up. David Horner, who was a life-long companion to Osbert Sitwell, used to come. He was a tall, effete figure. The young Beth Chatto was often present, quietly absorbing this unique garden. I was a friend of hers, and of her brother Seeley. We would walk behind Cedric and John listening to risqué stories about plants – I learned a lot about plants and many other things. The conversation was racy and extraordinarily sophisticated. At 4.00 pm, Lucy Harwood, a neighbouring artist who acted as a sort of hostess to Cedric and Lett, rang a handbell to summon everyone for mugs of tea and rock cakes.

The conversation was racy and extraordinarily sophisticated.

We all went to fancy dress parties at the house in Colchester of Dr Bob Sauvan-Smith and his friend Peggy Kirkaldy. Bob bought a number of Cedric's pictures and paid many visits. Among the artists who came were Joan Warburton (Maudie), one of Cedric's early pupils at Dedham, and Richard Chopping and Denis Wirth-Miller were part of the circle at this time. Nigel Scott, nicknamed 'The Bird', became Cedric's companion during the 1950s. He was a fine gardener and together they opened up the top garden at Benton End. He transformed Cedric's life in some ways but, tragically, he died

Cedric Morris: *Majorca Daja*, 1944. Oil on canvas. 60 x 48 cm. Minories.

The greatest crime at Benton End was to be boring!

some years later while he and Cedric were plant-hunting in Madeira.

The tuition at Benton End was based rather on the Parisian atelier style – sitting at the feet of the master kind of thing. There were no formal lessons or lectures and students were encouraged to place their easels all over the garden. Cedric and Lett had lived in Newlyn after the first world war, and there was a feeling of Cornwall in the colour of the house and a definite whiff of the Mediterranean in the food and wine. The atmosphere was one of intellectual freedom. Everything was discussed. It was Bohemian in the best sense. Lett and Cedric were open about their homosexuality at a time when it was illegal to have such a relationship and they also conducted a fight against the philistinism of their day. The whole atmosphere was exciting and liberating.

Cedric had old-fashioned manners, was radical in his outlook and he didn't give a damn what people thought about him. He abhorred London and the art world. He was affectionate, unpretentious and never boring. The greatest crime at Benton End was to be boring! He had some close women friends but in general he didn't like women much and he used to say some dreadful things about them. He did nothing to promote his career – it was Lett who did that – but he knew his own worth. He was extremely disciplined in his working habits and toiled very hard at both his painting and his gardening. He didn't do a thing in the house and was oblivious to domestic practicalities. He never had much money. He never left the garden to walk down the High Street in Hadleigh – it was Lett who adminstered the school, did the shopping and cooking and the book-keeping. Lett was a good artist whose work was much influenced by Gaudier-Brzeska but his life was much taken up by running the Benton End household to the detriment of his work. The school closed in the winter when Cedric travelled in Europe and collected plants and Lett went 'for economy reasons' to Brown's Hotel in London!

I visited the house often and became loved and trusted by Cedric and Lett. They always thought of me as very young. The last time I saw Cedric I'd been to Sizewell beach with Glyn Morgan. We were both caught in torrential rain. I hung my jeans over the Aga, and Millie, the housekeeper, fetched me an ancient three-piece suit of Cedric's – which I wore to supper – without a shirt!

Cedric was blind at the end of his life and would lie in the sun like an old cat. His wonderful garden had turned into a hayfield with the exotics he had collected towering over the grass.

Cedric's work is beginning to be more seriously acknowledged now as truly original. He had a curious method of starting to paint from the top corner of the picture. He used an earthy but sumptuous palette. He loved painting birds and his portraits have been described as 'shrieking likenesses'. The lasting influence that Benton End had on me was a sense of openness, honesty and intellectual freedom. Not to give a damn!

The lasting influence that Benton End had on me was a sense of openness, honesty and intellectual freedom.

The following article 'Sir Cedric Morris' is from People *edited by Susan Hill, Chatto & Windus, 1983 and is reprinted here by kind permission of the author.*

The notion that he changed somebody else's life would not have appealed to Cedric Morris, and he certainly cannot be said to have changed mine. Not in any full, re-directed sense, that is. Yet it would not be as it is now without him. Not quite. Our meeting not long after the war, myself very young and he entering upon the first of his various stages of a coherent, beautiful oldness, introduced a whole range of new attitudes and ideas to my existence which gave it just the right amount of carelessness it needed in order to survive. But no actual advice or preaching, needless to add. Just an unapologetic display of hedonism and regular work which said: go and do thou likewise. Why not? Quite a lot of artists and writers in the Suffolk villages all around were saying much the same thing, but Cedric Morris, with

Cedric Morris: *Jinny Leacock*, 1945. Oil on canvas. 61 x 46 cm. Minories.

... one was forever discovering past inter-connections.

his own beginnings rooted in an especially attractive wilfulness, said it most eloquently. When he died in February 1982, after a curious sliding tumble through his overcoat to the brick floor on which we met thirty years ago, I thought, now there must be a gap, a great vacancy, the shattering of the first circle. But no, and for the simple reason that when people are in their nineties, as Cedric was, they stop taking up the full human space. 'He's not all there!' the village boys used to shout at some persecuted creature of their own age, and for some months past it was plain to me that, although he was in his chair at dinner, or trotting down the black staircases at Benton End, or cutting into the talk with all the old amusement and relevance, vital aspects of Cedric had already wandered off on their own devices, leaving us just enough of his personality to trick us into thinking that he was still all there and could be for ever.

He knew differently. Last Christmas, when the first deep snow had fallen, he said to me, 'Do they touch your sleeve like this?' giving a little attention-drawing pluck to his jacket. Well, they don't, to be honest. Not yet. But if I manage to live to be ninety I dare say they will. Except for being almost blind – we said our names as we kissed him – and except for having to let his beard grow in a blossom-white fringe, he had altered hardly at all. When we pieced together the ancient photograph albums he had torn up, the images of his early self grinned through the rents, proving that time had only done the expected surface damage, nothing more. The long-lastingness of the incorrigible element in him was particularly obvious.

I was taken to Benton End for the first time by James Turner, a poet who had come to live on the Suffolk borders in order to write and grow mushrooms. I remember the day vividly. It marked not only the meeting with Cedric but also my first understanding of the nature of the local artists and writers, viewed as a group. First that it was not a coterie in the St Ives sense, second that it was linked together with much historic subtlety, so that one was forever discovering past inter-connections. In any case, James Turner's friendship with Cedric, like that of John Nash and many more, was based more on horticulture than art and literature, and after a brief taking stock of me, Cedric led us out into the celebrated brilliance of his 'iris week', and I was initiated into a realm of flowers, botanical and art students, earthy-fingered grandees and a great many giggly asides which I didn't quite get. He had just inherited his father's baronetcy and this seemed to add to the comedy. The gardeners wove their way round easels propped up in the long grass and the artists, of all ages, painted peering visitors and dense foliage in the exuberant Morris manner. The doors and window-frames of the ancient house glared Newlyn blue and there was a whiff of garlic and wine in the air from distant kitchens. The atmosphere was well out of this world so far as I had previously witnessed and tasted it. It was robust and coarse, and exquisite and tentative all at once. Rough and ready and fine mannered. Also faintly dangerous.

'Well,' asked James Turner, as we drove home, 'what did you think?'

I thought I had never seen anything like it, the big scrubbed table and the wooden platters, the cool ochre room crammed with lustre and bold oils of seabirds, formidable women fatiguing the salad and discussing plants, knowing youths, candlelight and marmalade cats (one of the women was Kathleen Hale), wine, a single-bar electric fire sputtering before an eighteenth-century bread oven and an overall feeling of spartan grandeur. This last impression owed much to Lett, who had lived with Cedric since 1919, and who was also an artist. It was Lett who actually ran the school of art, complaining mightily, though always producing from a chaotic kitchen the most delicious food and drink. Nor did his contribution end there, for having placed it before us – their meals in the gaunt Suffolk bakehouse were curiously stately – he immediately took up his next role, that of story-teller. The tales were either scandalously about himself or floridly about their travels and encounters, and were designed to shock and inform. If his facts were often inexact, his gist was transparent. Occasionally Cedric would step in and straighten our some curly bit of tale without condemnation or fuss, or with one of his bouts of glee. Lett talked through a big wicked smile like the wolf-grandmother in Little Red Riding Hood. With his large frame and rearing, scarred

Lett talked through a big wicked smile like the wolf-grandmother in Little Red Riding Hood.

… he made no bones about dominating the scene.

Cedric Morris: *Cafe Scene*, 1921.

bald dome, a legacy from the Western Front, and his mocking courtesy, he made no bones about dominating the scene. Much, much later, sitting with him during his last illness, at ease and fond of him, I tasted little surges of regret about my early self which, contrary to what was generally believed, was neither prim nor charmingly shy, but steely in that non-giving sense in which the young frequently are steely. But even then, as the pair of old friends complained their way out of a world which they had taken every advantage of, and which they had greedily enjoyed, I still found difficulty in telling either one of them, and it should have been Cedric, how grateful I was that they had deflected me from too much safety.

It was inevitable that I should become the Benton End scribe, especially as Cedric's notion of written information was one wobbly line on a postcard, and Lett's was as following:

> Cedric was born, of phenomenal vitality, on December 10th 1889. He was the eldest child of George Lockwood Morris of Sketty, Glamorgan (who, according to Burke, was descended from Owen Gwynedd, the last Prince of North Wales) … Bored and nonconformist in his father's household he made off to Canada. There he worked as a hired man on ranches in Ontario where the farmers seem rather to have taken advantage of his unusual energy and his naif ignorance of standard wages in the New World … Eighteen months later, he seems to have been studying singing at the Royal College of Music under Signor Vigetti, whose attempts at raising his light baritone to a tenor were unsuccessful. He determined to study painting in Paris.
>
> … In Paris he industriously attended all the available *croquis libre* classes at the Académies la Grande Chaumière and Collarossi; Académie Moderne (under Othon Friesz, André Lhote and, later Fernand Léger); and was one of the first to enrol at the Académie Suédoise …

And so on, through gaudy Mediterranean travels, Cedric's membership of the London Group and the Seven and Five (seven painters and five sculptors), his hand in founding the Welsh Contemporary Art

Cedric Morris: *Portino de Aridida, Tenerife*, 1957. Oil on canvas. 54.5 x 75 cm. Minories.

Exhibitions between the wars, the settling down in Suffolk and the post-war plant-hunting, painting winter travels, which I also vividly remember, and finally Lett's attributing to his friend 'an unprecedented breadth of palette', whatever that might mean. But the herald-like proclamation with its emphatic Gallicisms is mentioned because it contrasted so completely with Cedric's own version of events, not in detail but in tone. The past was all a bit of a mumble to him. If you listened hard you might be lucky and catch a glimpse of it, but no sweep of scene and wilful goings-on, and heightened in French, as with Lett. The reason was simple. Cedric was a pagan who liked the sun on his back and the day's colours in his eyes, and the tastes and sounds of Now. On a really beautiful afternoon at Benton End he could be seen lurking amidst the vast blooms he had brought to Suffolk from all over the world, virtually hugging the Now to him, his

Cedric was a pagan who liked the sun on his back and the day's colours in his eyes ...

Cedric Morris: *Landscape Azores*, 1966. Oil on canvas. 77 x 56 cm. Private collection.

Although so unlike him, I was drawn easily into his conspiracy of laughing judgements and solid work …

brown old face tilted a little skywards and his person defyingly, or helplessly elegant in the brown old clothes. A tour through the beds was learned and hilarious by turns, Cedric himself becoming quite convulsed by the habits of some plants and people. It was a curiously unoffending mix-up of sweetness and malice, a cocking a snook at conventions which had wilted long ago, due partly no doubt to earlier such naughty responses to them. Contrasting quite overwhelmingly with this merriment was a seriousness about art and humanity which had a way of pulling one up, of forcing one to be entirely truthful about what one said next. The passing in turn of brilliant specialist information (usually about botany), ideas on painting, escatology, wisdom, period camp and the most memorable individual-respecting tenderness created the kind of mercurial atmosphere which I – all of us – never quite got accustomed to. It was, of course, a perfectly unselfconscious bravura language belonging to the old bohemianism.

I was intrigued and entranced by Cedric's creature-like satisfaction with present time. It made his days so expansive that although he was visited to an alarming extent, an enormous amount of painting and gardening went on, apparently without interruption. When he was ninety he cursed God, whom he still took to be some ghastly Sunday misery from Glamorgan, for 'insulting' him with old age, but his sensuous basking in what pleasurable little treats each hour might provide continued to the last. Nobody has such a good time as a good-time puritan. Although so unlike him, I was drawn easily into his conspiracy of laughing judgements and solid work, although, alas, I was too much myself to achieve anything approaching his freedom.

He had exhibited regularly since the early twenties, with Lett and Gaudier-Brzeska in New York in 1926, with Ben and Winifred Nicholson, Christopher Wood (whom he taught), Ivon Hitchens, John Piper and the other members of the Seven and Five during the thirties, and both Wales and Suffolk had recently mounted retrospectives, but few artists could have done less to put their work on view. Seen standing amidst his landscapes, portraits ('not speaking but shrieking likenesses', as Raymond Mortimer called them), and flower pieces, the latter absolutely magnificent, a confrontation by vegetable hue and texture, shape and one almost adds scent which were nothing less than Cedric's notion of being alive in the world on a bright day, he acquired a quite awesome dimension which made even those of us who nursed white and ginger cats with him before the bar-fire hold back a bit. Standing beside him would be Millie Gomersall [Haines], his housekeeper for many years, ex-Fitzrovian and friend of the poet David Gascoyne during his pre-war Paris days, and herself restored to a kind of state by the unaccustomed finery which both she and Cedric had donned for the occasion. Although so countrified, Cedric retained much of the cosmopolitanism which Paris and Fitzrovia had given him. He perched in cities – 'When you took a room in Percy Street, you never asked for anything more than a table, a chair and a bed' – but luxuriated in an open landscape.

When the Tate Gallery celebrates him, it will be odd to stand amidst what will be the longest account of British post-Impressionism, as a single artist can give it, and not have it dominated by that rangy figure with its soft voice being so courteous and so improper by turn. Staring down at us will be, not only the company we shared at Benton End but the company before we existed, Anna Wickham, John Banting, Anthony Butts, Keidrich Rhys, Lucian Freud (his pupil), Rosamund Lehmann, Archie Gordon, Richard Chopping and Penelope-Keith-faced women with names like Mrs Byng-Stamper. And the earthy Cedric geography of Umbria, Cornwall, Brittany, the Algarve, Mexico and Suffolk, none of it remote or exotic any longer, although in even the paintings of the sixties there is a quality which suggests that such areas of daily light and air and absorbing work take some getting to. Between the heads and the places will be the famous twenties birds, ravens, shags and herons, and everywhere his flowers, opulent, glorious, yet even at their most blazingly coloured and translucent, rooted in the soil which he had pressed around them. 'Not a boring thing,' was his ultimate accolade – rarely bestowed – when he was shown a friend's garden, and it was what he managed never to have in his life if he could help it, a boring thing.

Cedric Morris: *Plant Designs*, 1922. Indian ink and watercolour. 25 x 35 cm. Minories.

Although so countrified, Cedric retained much of the cosmopolitanism which Paris and Fitzrovia had given him.

Index

Aldridge, John 112
Allen, Janet 97–8, 99

Bacon, Francis 44, 52, 124
Banbury, Boo Boo 64
Banting, John 158
Bawden, Edward 115, 139
Beckett, Jack 63
Bedford, Celia 25
Berlin, Isaiah 51
Bevan, Bobbie 64
Bevan, Natalie 64, 111, 118
Blakiston, Mildred 43
Blythe, Ronald 114, 149–58
Bodman, Elizabeth *see* Wright, Elizabeth
Bonny, Fiona 99–101
Britten, Benjamin 52, 149
Broadley, Denise 23–5, 29, 46
Brooke, Bryan 19, 52, 81, 140
Brooks, Alan 128
Brown, Bernard 65–71
Burton, Colonel 67
Butts, Anthony 158

Carpenter, Ellis 49–52, 63, 67
Carr, Barbara 64
Carr, David 23, 29, 30, 64
Carrington, Dora 9
Carrington, Joanna 131–3
Carrington, Noel 131
Catlin, Professor 65
Caulfield, Patrick 127
Chase, Michael 79–81
Chatto, Andrew 84, 85
Chatto, Beth 47, 83–91, 96, 110, 114, 124, 136, 150
Chopping, Richard 27–8, 44, 47, 150, 158
Churchill, Randolph 52, 111
Clark, Daphne 117–19
Coghill, Anne 135–6
Constable, Ernest 46
Constable, John 39
Curl, Henley 64

Davey, Robert 63–4, 67
David, Elizabeth 4, 45, 88, 103, 106, 124, 130
Derain, André 39
Drewry, Yvonne 127

Elizabeth, Queen (*later* the Queen Mother) 89
Epstein, Jacob 53
Epstein, Kitty 46
Ericksson, Ashe 137–8
Evans, Bernard 46

Fisher, Renata 46
Freud, Lucian 9–10, 24, 27–8, 30, 46, 69, 118, 124, 140, 147, 158
Friesz, Othon 155
Frost, John 27

Gale, George 44
'Gas-oven Kate' 19
Gascoyne, David 158
Gaudier-Brzeska, Henri 151, 157
Gilligan, Barbara 23
Girling, Arthur 70
Goossens, Annie 46
Gordon, Archie 114, 158
Gordon-Forbes, Jasmine 36
Grainger, Esther 46
Greenwood, Arthur 65
Grierson, Mary 91
Guggenheim, Peggy 9

Hale, Kathleen 29–30, 46, 52, 53–7, 64, 111, 154
Orlando's Home Life 57
Orlando's Silver Wedding 56
Portrait of Lett Haines 55
Hambling, Maggi 9–10, 67, 96, 127–30
Cedric 96
Harwood, Lucy 17–18, 23, 25, 43, 46, 47, 49, 52, 64, 67, 106, 117, 128, 130, 140, 144, 146, 150
Hayes, Millie 43–4, 46, 52, 67, 73, 91, 96, 101, 104, 105, 118, 119, 158
Henie, Sonja 67

Hines, Maurice 63
Hinge and Bracket 119
Hitchens, Ivon 9, 157
Hodgkins, Frances 9, 67–9
Horner, David 150
'Hot-Handed Hetty' or 'The Royal Bum' 19, 67
Hunter, Kathleen 88

Innes, J.D. 9

John, Augustus and Dorelia 53

Keay, David 46
Kirkaldy, Peggy 150

Laing, Basil 110
Law, Aileen 59–60
Lees, Derwent 9
Léger, Fernand 39, 155
Lehmann, Rosamund 158
Leigh Fermor, Patrick 118
Lett Haines, Arthur
Angry Humble 54
Brighton Station 3
bronze head, by Bernard Reynolds 5
Fat Laugh 130
Composition 48
Congrès sur l'oeil 27
Conjectures 147
Escape, The 59
Incantation or Sabbat 105
Jardin d'artiste 135
Lion Hunt, The 76
Martyrdom of Purple Hampton, The 70
Pigmy Pouter Pigeons 33
Poor Dolly 68
Pour decouvrir le mystère de la Femme, tirez le masque 81
Regardant 127
Studies for Dragon's Mate 69
Two Figures 117
Vereda Tropicale 121
Witch Fetish: Portrait of Maggi Soop 129

Lhote, André 155
Lilley, Ted 63
Lloyd, Michael 121–5
Longford, Lord 140
Lungren, Eric 27

McCormick, Eric 68–9
Marrable, Rose 77
Mason, Christopher 131
Matisse, Henri 39
Maufe, Sir Edward 41
Maufe, Liz 41
Mayo, Eileen 140
Millais, J. Everett 41
Millard, Pat 135
Minton, John 135
Moore, Henry 33
Morgan, Con 135
Morgan, Glyn 15–21, 46, 73, 140, 152
  Species Irises 17
Morley, John 113–15
Morphet, Richard 81
Morris, Armin 122–4
Morris, Cedric
  Benton Blue Tit title page
  Blue Poppy, The 90, 93
  bronze head, by Bernard Reynolds 4
  Cabbages 41
  Cacti, Sedums and Succulents 100
  Café Rotonde 15
  Café Scene 78, 155
  Crisis 67
  Daya Majorca 44
  Denise Broadley 23
  Dragonmouth 133
  Easter Bouquet 87
  Fascists in Rome 9
  Garden Benton End 12, 18
  Golden Auntie 99
  Gutted Art School 2
  Helen Robbins 7
  Iris, Poppies and Clematis 31, 103
  Irises 16
  Irises Heralding 75
  Landscape at Newlyn 122
  Landscape Azores 157
  Llangynofor Bridge 123
  Lucy Harwood 25
  Majorca Daja 151
  Minton Pot, The 37
  Mixed Flowers 63
  Nemesis 8
  Paysage du Jardin 51
  Plant Design 35
  Plant Designs 158
  Portimao, Algarve 114
  Portino de Aridida, Tenerife 156
  Portrait of Eva Douglas 6
  Pound Farm 143
  Quinces and Nerines 60, 118
  Red Hot Pokers 20
  Red Wing and Mistle Thrush 107
  River Brett, Hadleigh vi
  St Helena 110
  Standing Nude (two with same title) 124, 136
  Still Life 95
  Still Life before Sussex Fireback 109, 119
  Still Life with Courgettes and Tomatoes 28
  Succulents in Schnake's Pot 83
  Tom Wright 145
  Wartime Garden 1
  Woman with Earrings 148
  Wood Pigeons 73, 141
Morris, George Lockwood 155
Morris, Henry 122
Morris, Robert 122
Mortimer, Raymond 157
Mount, Frances 103–7
Munnings, Alfred 4, 23

Nash, John 9, 24, 43, 47, 64, 96, 112, 114, 140, 149–50, 153
Neve, Christopher 109
Nicholson, Ben and Winifred 9, 157
Nolan, Sidney 119
Norris Wood, John 139–41

Ogilvie, Patrick 47
O'Malley, Maudie *see* Warburton, Joan

Pears, Peter 52
Picasso, Pablo 39, 79
Piper, John 69
Platts Mills, John 65

Pond, Frank 36, 59–61

Reynolds, Bernard 33–9, 43, 46, 60
Reynolds, Gwynneth 41–4
Rhys, Keidrich 158
Richards, Ceri 15
Robinson, Jenny 93–6, 110
Roper, Primrose 103
Russell, Rosemary 140
Russell-Smith, Mollie 27–31, 46

Sackville-West, Vita 96, 111, 150
Sauvan-Smith, Bob 150
Scott, Nigel 47, 69, 83, 84, 88, 91, 94, 150–1
Shelton, Hattie 46
Sitwell, Osbert 150
Skeaping, John 24, 29, 114, 115, 118
Smart, Elizabeth 97, 113
Smith, Bob 64
Smith, Matthew 29, 39
Spencer, Stanley, work of 130
Spraggons, Ronnie 63
Stewart, Gerry 75
Styles, Lorna 47
Suddaby, Rowland 43

Thornton, Valerie (*later* Chase) 79, 81
Turner, James 149, 153–4

van Horn, Count and Countess 147
Venison, Tony 109–12, 114
Vigetti, Signor 155

Wakefield, Felicity 77–8
Wakefield, Peter 75–6, 77, 78
Warburton, Joan (*later* O'Malley) 25, 29, 43, 81, 111, 140, 150
Waters, Derek 45–8, 49, 63, 67, 69
Watling, W.T. 59
White, Trevor 63
Wickham, Anna 158
Wilde, Oscar, memorial to 127
Wirth-Miller, Dennis 27–8, 44, 150
Wood, Christopher 9, 140, 157
Wright, Elizabeth (*née* Bodman) 43, 46, 47, 51, 143–8
Wright, Tom(my) 43, 46, 47, 51, 67, 70–1, 147, 148

Yeames, W.F. 41

Zadkine, Ossip 39